Graphic design by Angela C. Park
Cover photographs by Lisa Mullenneaux

ISBN: 0-9704296-1-4
Library of Congress Card Number: 00-192089

To order copies, send $9.95 plus $2.00 shipping to:
The Penington Press
PO Box 829
New York, NY 10009-9998

VERMONT ANTIQUING:

SIX DAY TRIPS

by Lisa Mullenneaux

THE PENINGTON PRESS
NEW YORK, NY

VERMONT ITINERARIES

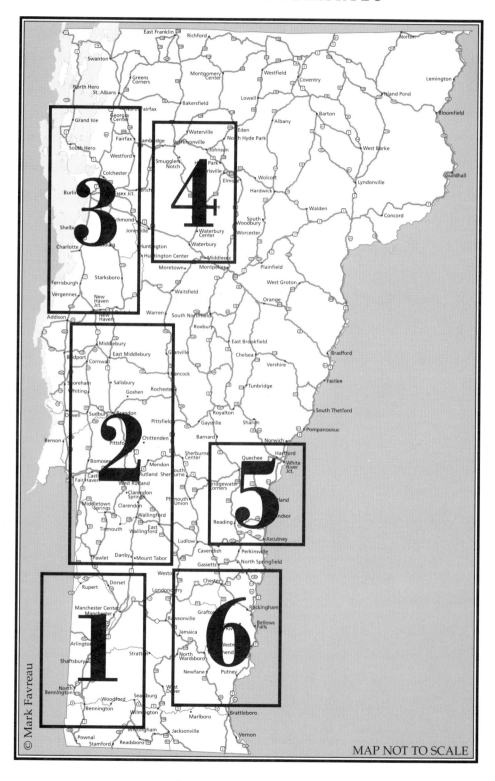

© Mark Favreau

MAP NOT TO SCALE

CONTENTS

INTRODUCTION: Of Whimsies, Weathervanes, and   **1**
Windsor Chairs

ITINERARY 1:   Bennington to Dorset   **7**
via routes 7, 7A, and 30
Miles: 35

ITINERARY 2:   Danby to Middlebury   **25**
via routes 7, 140, 133, and 4
Miles: 67

ITINERARY 3:   Vergennes to Burlington   **41**
via route 7
Miles: 25

ITINERARY 4:   Waterbury to Stowe   **57**
via routes 100, 15, and 108
Miles: 56

ITINERARY 5:   Quechee to Reading   **69**
via routes 4, 12, and 106
Miles: 23

ITINERARY 6:   Chester to South Newfane   **83**
via routes 35, 121, and 30
Miles: 42

APPENDICES: What Exactly is an Antique?   **99**
Sleuthing Country Furniture   **101**
Beginning a Book Collection   **102**
Tales of Antiques "Pickers"   **104**
Annual Antiques Shows   **107**
Travel Resources   **108**
Dealer Quick Reference Guide   **111**
Index to Towns by Itinerary   **115**

OF WHIMSIES, WEATHERVANES, AND WINDSOR CHAIRS

Antiquing has become a passionate sport in the Green Mountain state—in all seasons, for all ages. Buyers are not only more numerous, but more savvy, and dealers have sprung up to meet them. In 10 years, the number of fulltime antiques dealers has grown 30 percent, according to Peter Pill, owner of Grafton Gathering Place and former president of the Vermont Antiques Dealers' Association (VADA). He estimates part-time dealers have doubled or even tripled.

With such a wide selection, the challenge for today's antiques treasure-hunter is no longer where to search but how to search most effectively. Everyone—at least according to his store shingle—sells antiques. How do the uninitiated separate the vintage "junque" from items with age and value, museum-quality pieces with five-figure price tags from pieces a novice collector might be able to afford?

This guide is the answer and, like most guides, its purpose is to save you time. It's the result of many hours of prospecting the antiques trail, hours made even more enjoyable because Vermont is designed to be explored by car. Road signs with easy-to-read directions and mileage point motorists to antiques dealers, inns, and restaurants hidden from view off the main highway. Information centers along the way provide travel brochures, maps, and other prospectors' tools. Best of all, Vermonters prefer their mountain vistas uncluttered by billboards .

Still it helps to do your homework before you hit the road. In

1

planning a trip, I rely on VADA's directory of members and regional antiques brochures to locate dealers in a particular area. Then I check to see if those dealers have Websites, which gives me more information about their wares, and how and when to reach them. These "virtual tours" are good preparation for the real thing. When I've mapped out an itinerary, I book inn reservations and make appointments with those dealers who request them. Then I pray for clear weather.

When I first began collecting, I remember reasoning: hey, if I don't pay much for an item and it turns out to be worthless, it won't matter. It *always* matters. So the first step to serious collecting is to buy from reliable dealers. Auctions and flea markets can be fun—if you have the time—but caveat emptor. They offer no guarantees that the piece sold is the genuine article. Believe me, if you invest $1200 in a deacon's bench and a chatty neighbor points out that the wood may be old but it came off the side of a barn, you will want the option of returning it.

VADA members are required to accept returned items within 60 days if a customer can prove that the item is other than the dealer warranted. "Because of the range in what people collect these days, VADA is more concerned with integrity," president Elizabeth Harley told me, "than with how old the piece is. We ask our members to stand behind what they sell and to share as much information as they can." They must clearly mark items as to date and condition (that means any repair or restoration). Furniture made after 1900, for example, must be so marked and displayed in a separate space.

The second step to serious collecting is to buy the best you can afford. As long as you buy wisely—not on impulse—that redware bowl or powder horn will have increased its value when you want, or need, to sell it. But antiques are more than an investment; they have fascinating stories to tell us. That redware bowl once sat on a farmer's kitchen table, the powder horn might have been used by one of Ethan Allen's Green Mountain Boys in Revolutionary War skirmishes. Each played a unique part in the folk life of New England. Thus, the antiques we live with day to day link us to the past in profoundly satisfying ways.

One final word: I have found that some of the state's best dealers don't advertise and often request an appointment. Don't be put off by that request nor by the need to abandon the highway for a side trip up a rutted mountain road. These dealers have chosen their locations for their physical beauty and part of the fun of backroads antiquing is seeking them out (as long as they know you are coming). Their homes are usually as unique as their collections, each with its distinctive personality. Many dealers enjoy sharing their knowledge of the trade with visitors and some are memorable storytellers. It all enhances the experience of antiquing in Vermont.

Happy prospecting!

HOW TO USE THIS GUIDE

These road trips are intended to be covered in a day, and the itineraries are changeable, depending on your interests. They form a rough circle clockwise from Bennington north to Burlington east to Quechee and south to Newfane, making it easy to return west on route 9 to Bennington for a complete loop. Needless to say, the loop can be reversed. Each itinerary is preceded by a map indicating distance between shops and followed by suggestions for places to eat and stay overnight. (Be sure to travel with the latest Vermont map, available from www.travel-vermont.com) Each itinerary ends with space for a "travel diary," where you can record items you either have bought or might buy in future. I like to paperclip a shop's business card to the page.

If you have suggestions for improving the guide or comments about your shopping, dining, or overnight experiences, please let us know. We want to know how to make your "antiques roadshow" as memorable as possible.

The area code for all phone numbers is 802, unless otherwise indicated. "By appointment only" in a dealers' listing means that a phone call is required. "By chance or appointment" means that a phone call is recommended.

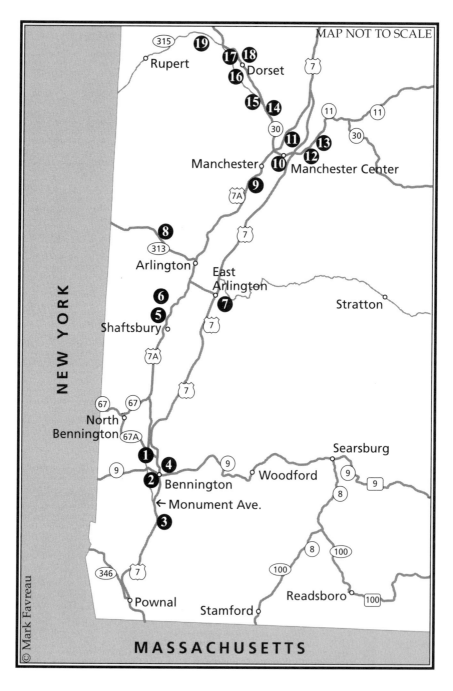

MAP NOT TO SCALE

NEW YORK

MASSACHUSETTS

315

⑲ Rupert

⑰ ⑱
⑯ Dorset

7

⑮ ⑭

30

11 11

30

⑪ ⑬
⑫
Manchester ⑩ Manchester Center

⑨ 7A

7

⑧

313

Arlington

East
Arlington
⑦

Stratton

⑥
⑤

Shaftsbury

7A

7

7

67 67

North
Bennington 67A

① ④
9 ② 9 Woodford
Bennington
← Monument Ave.
③

9

Searsburg

9
9
8

8 100

346 7

100

Pownal

Stamford

8

Readsboro 100

6

Itinerary 1

BENNINGTON TO DORSET
by routes 7, 7A, and 30
Miles: 35

Vermont was wilderness long after its neighbors—New York and Massachusetts—were being settled in the 1600s and early 1700s. Bennington, being close to these colonies, was the first town chartered in 1749, and its rich history makes it the natural starting place for a driving tour of the state. By the mid-1800s, Bennington was famous as a pottery-making center. Today it is the center of several fine antiques shops and the gateway to a north-south pilgrimage that antiques devotees liken to the Yellow Brick Road. Once out of city traffic, scenic route 7A follows the valley north between the Taconic range to the west and the Green Mountains (the state's namesake) to the east.

Begin at the intersection of routes 7 and 9 in the heart of downtown Bennington. If you head west on route 9 about 1/2 mile, on your left is **(1) THE BENNINGTON MUSEUM**. For the serious collector, there is no better introduction to Vermont antiques than the furniture, decorative arts, and fine arts on display in these galleries. There are excellent examples of Old Bennington pottery, early American silver and glass, Revolutionary War artifacts, and 18th- and 19th-century American paintings and sculpture. There's even a treat for classic car fans: the Wasp, a sleek 1925 touring car designed and built in Bennington. The museum also owns the largest public collection of paintings by folk artist Grandma Moses. Her one-room schoolhouse, donated to the museum by her family, exhibits highlights of her life and work. 447-1571. Daily 9-5 Nov-May, 9-6 June-Oct. Closed Thanksgiving, Christmas, and New Year's. www.benningtonmuseum.com.

Continue driving west and the road will curve sharply to the left, where Monument Ave. crosses route 9. Turn left onto Monument Ave. This one-way street passes in front of Old First Church, behind which Robert Frost and other famous Vermonters rest in peace. Follow Monument Ave. south about 1/2 mile to the sign for **(2) STONEWALLS ANTIQUES** on your left. Jim and Gloria Lernihan's shop is in the back of their white, ranch-style house. They specialize in early American furniture in cherry and pine; unusual decorative accessories such as flow blue, cranberry, and amberina; and American and English silver smalls. Samplers decorate the walls, including—when I was last there—a set cross-stitched in 1824 by two English sisters. Most days May thru Dec. 10-5. 447-1628. http://stonewalls.safeshopper.com. VADA.

Continue driving south on Monument Ave. several miles until

"When you are making a dealer an offer, never say 'I'll give you....' Instead say 'Would you consider?' And remember that if a piece is too perfect, it's probably a reproduction." Jim Lernihan

it intersects with route 7. Turn right and **(3) FONDA'S ANTIQUES** is about a 1/2 mile on your left. Susan Church and her cousin Richard Bump are the latest owners of a family business that dates to 1927. Rustic pieces—Conestoga wagon stays, bottles, trunks, and cupboards—are stored in a barn and roadside stand. The main house displays a large variety of early stoneware in the Bennington Room, ample glass and china, quilts, textiles, and collectibles. About 50 percent of their large inventory is furniture. Daily 10-5. 442-5985.

"My cousin and I learned this trade as children working alongside our grandmother. She ran the shop for 50 years and knew some of the original Bennington potters. She was always proud of her large collection of their stoneware." Richard Bump

Now turn north on route 7 and drive back through downtown Bennington (about 1 1/2 miles) until it crosses County St. **(4) FOUR CORNERS EAST, INC.,** is tucked away on the right and easy to miss. But you wouldn't want to do that. Russ Bagley's gallery boasts an endlessly changing stock of American and Continental furniture, paintings, and accessories. Among the exotic items Bagley has plucked from obscurity for some lucky customers are two doors—one Spanish 17th-century, carved and painted; the other from an 18th-century Mexican confessional. You'll see exquisite examples of British period furniture, such as a small Davenport desk in burled walnut and mahogany with eight side drawers, and American pieces, such as a late 19th-century partner's desk . Wed.-Mon. 10-5. 442-2612. VADA, AADLA member.

Eight miles north of Bennington on 7A, your next stop might be Lucinda Gregory's **(5) CHOCOLATE BARN** in Shaftsbury for country furniture and hand-dipped chocolates—an unbeatable combination. Proudly displayed on her porch is a horse-drawn sleigh, a shingle-maker's bench, and a doctor's buggy. Inside the restored 1842 sheep barn is Gregory's candy kitchen with 600 antique chocolate molds and 56 varieties of sweets. Unusual items on two floors include a back-service bar in chestnut and bass from a stage-coach inn in Pennsylvania, an early 12-foot-long toboggan with a gong bell, a barrelback corner cupboard, and a child's toy bureau in maple. Daily 9:30-5:30. 375-6928.

Also in Shaftsbury is one of the state's outstanding dealers, **(6) NORMAN GRONNING,** whose American furniture is one-of-a-kind. Expect to see unusual and rare New England pieces in their original condition, fine and folk art, and early American cooking iron, andirons, cranes, and firebacks. 375-6376. Please call for an appointment and get directions to the shop. www.erols.com/egronnin. VADA, AAAA member.

Three miles north of Shaftsbury, turn right off 7A onto Warm Brook Rd., go straight through the blinking traffic light, then right at Ice Pond Rd. You are in the hamlet of East Arlington and can park by the old mill stream. Above the Post Office, a sign on the **(7) EAST ARLINGTON ANTIQUES CENTER** reads: "Think that the world is moving too fast? Step upstairs and visit the past." Two group shops—within a five-minute walk of each other—are worth a side trip because the picturesque village here—with its mills and lovely green—is listed on the National Register of Historic Places. Owner Phil Elwell houses the stock of 125 dealers crowded into 12,000 square feet. His inventory includes Old Bennington pottery, tools, kitchenware, perfume and snuff bottles, books, linens, and some period furniture. Ask him about the pros and cons of multi-dealer shops like his own that have sprouted like mushrooms in every part of Vermont. For dealers, they mean greater exposure for a small rent, and for buyers, greater inventory to browse. Daily 9-5. 375-9607 and 375-6144.

"In 12 years, I've only had one item returned. It was a Currier and Ives lithograph, which turned out to be a reproduction." Phil Elwell

---

From East Arlington, head west on Route 313 towards Arlington. **(8) THE FARM ANTIQUES** has no sign out front; it doesn't need to advertise. Every Vermont dealer knows the quality of Jean and Gedeon LaCroix's collection of Americana. "It's a hobby gone wild," says Gedeon, who, in additon to being a hobbyist, serves as trustee emeritus of the Bennington Museum. Their 1820 farmhouse includes a taproom recreated from the Raleigh Tavern in Williamsburg, folk art, country pieces, and a livingroom full of cherry Chippendale chest of drawers and tables. All year. Please call for an appointment and directions to the shop. 375-6302. VADA member.

From Arlington, drive north on 7A about four miles. On the right next to the Weathervane Motel, Anne Alenick runs a small shop she calls **(9) PARAPHERNALIA.** She specializes in silver bibelots, which are tiny objects you can hold in the palm of your hand. She also likes to buy French and English paintings; art glass, such as Gallé; Oriental ivories and cloisonné; and Victorian jewelry. I admired some elegant snuff boxes and carving knife rests in glass and metal. Closed Nov. 1-May 20. 362-2421. VADA member.

As you enter Manchester Center on route 7A, look for **(10) COMOLLO ANTIQUES,** on the right next to Mother Myrick's Confectionery and Ice Cream Parlor. Barbara and Clarke Comollo reign over a quaint kingdom of musical instruments, high-end glass, garden ornaments, hand-painted porcelain, early iron, coin silver, oil paintings, and stoneware, all attractively arranged in their street shop. When I arrived, Clarke had just acquired an 1840 corner cupboard of mahogany, boxwood, and pine crafted by Hastings Warren from Middlebury, VT. Clarke picked up a book and showed me a similar piece, owned by the

Bennington Museum. I admired several French armoires, a New York mahogany table over 13 feet long; a Vermont-made, grain-painted case clock; a cast-iron flagpole eagle; an Art Deco serigraph poster; and an 1840 Italian marble-top table. This is an eclectic collection of top quality. Ask about

"We love what we're doing and enjoy helping our customers get what they want at a fair price." Clarke Comollo

their library of books on collecting, including hard-to-find imprints. All are for sale. Thur.-Tues. 10-5. www.vtantiques.com. 362-7188. VADA member.

Follow Historic Main St. (7A) through its "malfunction junction" with route 11/30. At the top of the hill turn right on Center Hill Rd. Follow it about 1/4 mile south to Jeff and Kathy Metzger's **(11) CENTER HILL PAST AND PRESENT**, a multidealer shop in a yellow renovated barn. The stained-glass window on the top floor that reads "Welcome" is not just for effect; this shop has a very welcoming presence and reasonable prices on a mix of old and made-to-look-old items. Jeff explained that he uses local craftspeople to make new pieces of furniture—like farm tables—out of old wood, but that he's careful to represent them as such in the store. Among the vintage pieces that intrigued me were a red Christmas sleigh priced at $895, an oak Frigid-brand ice box for $525, and a baby's pine bathtub with soapdish for $200. 362-3211. Daily 10-5 April-Dec.; weekends Jan.-March.

Continue south on Center Hill Rd. and turn left on Elm St. Next to Al Ducci's Italian take-out is **(12) JUDY PASCAL ANTIQUES,**

Judy Pascal with one of her signature canopy beds

where you can shop for country furniture and accessories; textiles; hooked, rag, and braided rugs; toleware; garden elements; quilts; and coverlets. One of Pascal's unusual talents is to create canopy beds using old architectural pieces. 362-2004. Daily 10-5. VADA member. www.judypascalantiques.com. Pascal shares the building with Shirley Maiden of Maiden Lane, who sells vintage women's clothing, drapes, duvets, and other bedding. 362-2004.

Just to be neighborly, you might meander into Neil Landres' **(13) MEANDER BOOKSHOP**. On the first floor of his Victorian house, you'll find a selection of first editions, leather-bound antiquarian volumes, maps (especially of New England), and newer books, all irrestible to bibliophiles. A transplanted New Yorker, Landres can persuade you to abandon the asphalt jungle for Vermont's open spaces. Summer: Thur.-Mon. 10-6. Call for winter hours. 362-0700.

Back at "malfunction junction," follow the signs for route 30 north, drive four miles, and you've entered the hamlet of Dorset. Three years ago Wendy and Mark Putnam bought the Lernihan's shop at Stonewall Lane and renamed it **(14) THE OLD COW'S TAIL ANTIQUES**. They favor country furniture, Sterling silver, glass, oil lamps, fine porcelain and china, and early tools, much of which is described on their Website. Some fun items include a fancy mahogany footwarmer, a lidded sewing box, and a rosewood humidor (for your best cigars). Daily 10-5. 362-3363. www.oldcowstailantiques.com. VADA member.

"We specialize in oil lamps of all varieties, priced from $150 to $800. We also collect etchings by Manchester artist Luigi Lucioni." Mark Putnam

---

If quilts strike your fancy, make your next stop **(15) MARIE MILLER AMERICAN QUILTS**, just past Putnams on the left. She has an international reputation for outstanding 19th- and early

20th-century American quilts in all sizes and price ranges. She also has a multipage Website where you can preview these "found treasures." Each quilt is dated and meticulously described as to condition, workmanship, and artistic appeal. It will set your mouth watering for the real thing and show you the range and quality of the 300-plus quilts she has in stock. They begin at about $195. She also sells hooked rugs, Quimper, and Bennington pottery, all of which you can order on the 'Net. Daily 10-5. 867-5969. www.antiquequilts.com VADA member.

The serenity of Dorset with its stately 19th-century buildings encircling a green may strike you as a welcome relief after Manchester's factory outlets and the traffic they attract. Park near the green and stretch your legs. One of three choice shops in the heart of the village, **(16) MIDDLESTONE ANTIQUES** has been owned by Bob and Anne August since 1995. They deal in Americana, folk art, country furniture, and rugs at very reasonable prices. I saw hooked rugs in good condition for $200-$300, an unusual 18-hole pewter candle mold circa 1836, and lots of decoys starting at $100. "Open if the flag is flying," says Anne or by appointment. 867-4448. Around the corner on the green, **(17) PEG AND JUDD GREGORY** sell museum-quality period and country furniture from the 17th- to the 19th-centuries, both American and English. They also display a wide selection of delft and brass. Wed-Sun 10-5. 867-4407. VADA member.

Opposite Dorset's village green, **(18) PHYLLIS CARLSON** specializes in textiles—such as hooked and braided rugs, quilts, needlepoint pillows and footstools, samplers, Victorian laces, and bedding—and figured wood furniture, such as tiger maple and

16

flame birch. Carlson started selling 25 years ago and gets most of her merchandise from families who seek her out. She has no trouble filling eight rooms with early American country and formal furniture, lighting, porcelain, and decorative accessories. I was immediately attracted to her Vermont coverlets, some of which are signed and dated. Daily 10-5 in summer. Call ahead in winter. 867-4510. VADA member.

> **"Anywhere you go in Vermont, there's a sleeper. But there aren't the bargains that there were even 10 years ago." Phyllis Carlson**

SIDETRIPS

Five miles west of the green in Dorset on route 315, Janet Fram and Bo Hermansen have a most unusual collection of Scandinavian furniture in their barns at **(19) COUNTRY GALLERY ANTIQUES.** These are early 19th-century armoires, tables, beds, sideboards, and stepbacks, stripped of their original paint, dried, sanded, and rubbed with wax. The result is called "scrubbed pine." I saw a sea captain's desk with a chart drawer and handles on each side for easy portability that Bo dated to 1820. Many of the armoires and cupboards were designed as "take-aparts" and could be moved in pieces. Essential because they are very heavy. Trestle tables are priced from $2000, armoires from $1000. Ask Bo about their intriguing histories. The Hermansen's also stock a selection of rag rugs, vintage lighting, enamelware, yelloware, and needlepoint.

17

Thur.-Sat. and Mon. 10-4. 394-7753. www.country-gallery.com. VADA member.

"I find original furniture in Denmark and Sweden and strip the paint off. Then we ship it to Vermont, where we sand and wax it. We could not duplicate the craftsmanship of these 150-year-old pieces and make a profit. They just don't make furniture like this anymore." Bo Hermansen

---

HILDENE is a 24-room Georgian Revival mansion, surrounded by formal gardens and panoramic views, built for Abraham Lincoln's only son Robert Todd Lincoln. Guided tours of the house and original furnishings are given daily on the half-hour from 9:30-4 mid-May through October. $8. 362-1788. Route 7A in Manchester Village.

PLACES TO STAY

ARLINGTON: Sherrie and Bill Noonan offer luxurious accommodations at the ARLINGTON INN, an 1848 Greek Revival mansion on route 7A. Twenty-two guestrooms, many with jacuzzis and fireplaces, range from $100-$265, and each is described on their Website (www.arlingtoninn.com). Dinners prepared by chef Jeff Scott range from $18.95-$26.95. The grounds are beautifully landscaped with gardens, patios, and ponds. Ask about their vacation packages. 375-6532 or 800 443-9442.

18

DORSET: CORNUCOPIA OF DORSET is a deluxe B&B in a restored 1880 colonial at 3228 route 30. Guests can choose from four rooms in the main house priced at $130-$165 or a cottage suite at $225-$245. Rooms feature poster or canopy beds, fireplaces, sitting areas, and private baths. Champagne check-in and candlelight breakfasts make this a popular choice for a romantic weekend. Innkeepers Trish and John Reddoch list availability on their Website www.cornucopiaofdorset.com. 867-5751 or 800 566-5751.

MANCHESTER VILLAGE: A former 20-acre Victorian estate, the Wilburton Inn surveys the Battenkill Valley from its quiet summit on River Rd. off route 7A. Sculptures and paintings throughout the house and grounds reflect owners Albert and Georgette Levis' commitment to the arts. Spacious guestrooms in the main house plus many cottage/suites range from $105-$250. Breakfast is served in the Terrace Room, dinner in the Billiard Room, afternoon tea in the Livingroom; pool swimming and tennis on the grounds. Ask about their special events packages. 362-2500 or 800 648-4944. www.wilburton.com.

PLACES TO EAT

BENNINGTON: THE BLUE BENN DINER may just serve the world's best breakfasts; at least it's a strong contender. Try the California Benedict, poached eggs topped with guacamole hollandaise and served with black beans. (Popeye's version is served over spinach.) Vegetarian specials, like "nut burgers," and a strict nonsmoking policy make it a most unusual diner. Open 6 a.m. daily except Sun. at 7 a.m. Around the corner from Four Corners East, Inc., on route 7. 442-5140.

MANCHESTER VILLAGE: If you want good grub in a cozy, pub-like setting, choose **MULLIGAN'S**. You can order pasta, steaks, and lighter fare for lunch and dinner at affordable prices. Their sports bar has six TV screens and over 60 types of beer. Route 7A across from the Manchester Inn. 362-3663.

MANCHESTER CENTER: Look for **MISTRAL'S AT TOLLGATE** five miles from the center of Manchester on Tollgate Rd. off route 11/30. The tollgate that originally stood in this spot is remembered in photos that decorate the walls. Today owner/chef Dana Markey serves French cuisine with dinner entrees that range from $19-$30; chateaubriand and rack of lamb for two cost a bit more. An exhaustive wine list. Open for dinner at 6. Reservations recommended. Closed Wed. July-Oct.; Closed Tues. and Wed. Nov-June. 362-1779.

TRAVEL DIARY

TRAVEL DIARY

TRAVEL DIARY

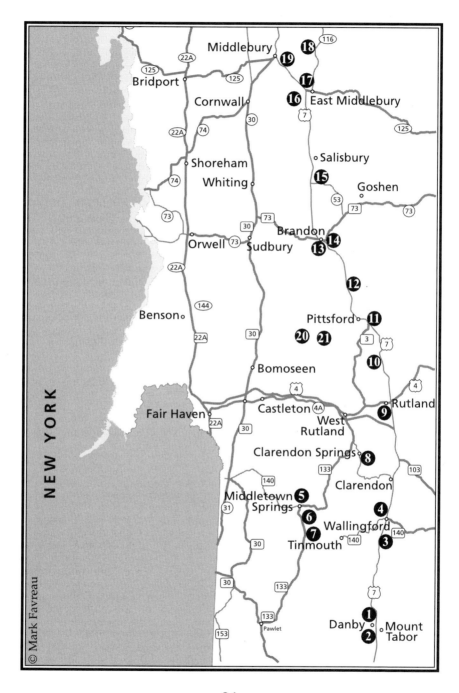

Itinerary 2

DANBY TO MIDDLEBURY
by routes 7, 140, 133, and 4
Miles: 67

To reach Danby from the south, you'll drive north on route 7 past majestic peaks with less-than-majestic names like Owl's Head, Buckball, and Mad Tom Notch. Take a deep breath of the pine-scented air as you pass mile after mile of hillsides forested in balsam, hemlock, and birch. It's a visually stunning drive with lots of opportunity for a quick hike, swim, or picture-taking. Equally scenic is the shortcut from Dorset over dirt-surfaced Danby Mountain Road. Turn right at Danby Four Corners and follow Mill Brook into Danby.

The village of Danby is just a crossroads really, but it is a favorite pit stop for antiquers because of Agnes Franks. Franks owns the **(1) DANBY ANTIQUES CENTER**, the oldest continuously operating antiques center in Vermont, and—unlike some groups shops where quality is uneven—its standards are exemplary. Early American furniture and accessories are arranged in spacious room settings in an 11-room Federal-style house. A barn contains newer items. The country pieces are priced to sell—coverlets from $150 to $250, a blanket chest in original green paint for $450, a stepback cupboard for $1000, and lots of banks—both mechanical and still—priced at $100 and up. My favorite? A Punch and Judy show, all ready to set up and play. This is a coop of quality dealers with one of the friendliest shop managers around. Daily 10-5 Apr.-Dec.. Call ahead for Tues.-Wed. hours Jan.-Mar. 293-5990. VADA member.

"We vet all our inventory, and any item less than 100 years old goes into the barn." Agnes Frank

---

If you like what you see at the Danby Antiques Center, you might want to walk six houses down So. Main St. and talk to Barbara and Brian Martin. They exhibit at the Center but have more stock in their shop at **(2) THE BARN ANTIQUES**. They can show you oil paintings and prints, jewelry, folk art, books, and whatever they've netted at auctions and estate sales. Barbara says "If we're not home, we're out looking for treasures." 293-5512. By chance or appointment.

Retrace your route to 7 and continue north towards Wallingford. One mile south of the village, Wayne and Eleanor Santwire sell a large selection of American country and formal furniture, accessories, primitives, and stoneware at **(3) COUNTRY**

HOUSE ANTIQUES. Their mid-1800s barn has been renovated to accommodate a variety of beds on the top floor—spools, four-posters, cannonballs, and brass and irons. Furniture on the bottom floor includes large and small pieces—armoires, cupboards, and chests. Items I spotted on my last visit were a nine-foot-long farm table in pine and birch circa 1870 and a 32-drawer map chest. You'll find reproductions mixed with originals here. Daily 10-5. 446-2344.

(4) OLD TYME SHOP ANTIQUES on route 7 in Wallingford is a treasure trove of valuable timepieces. Clayton Doty both sells and repairs European and American wall and shelf clocks. He can show you fine examples of grandfather, grandmother, black mantel, gingerbread, and schoolhouse clocks, all guaranteed to be original. By chance or appointment. 446-2828.

At the intersection with route 140, turn left and climb the hairpin turns over Tinmouth Mountain (about 10 miles) until you descend into Middletown Springs. It's well worth the journey. After 22 years in business, Janna Tornabene has made a name for herself selling fine Victorian and other 19th-century furniture and

27

Janna Tornabene owns Old Spa Shop Antiques

accessories at **(5) OLD SPA SHOP ANTIQUES.** A brick 1814 colonial known as the Jonas Clark House is the splendid setting for her collection, which—when I visited—included a Victorian sette in pale yellow brocade with a matching chair, several signed cabinet pieces, a recamier, a porcelain-lined cigar case, and an Empire six-drawer chest. By chance or appointment. 235-2366. VADA member.

Turn south on route 133 to find Alan L. Grace, aka **(6) THE CLOCK DOCTOR,** on the right just outside the village. If you make an appointment, he'll show you American and European restored clocks in tick-tock condition. 235-2440. VADA member. Neighbors Jim and Janet Webber specialize in early oil lamps and hanging lamps from 1700-1900. And they have hundreds of them as well as an assortment of antique match holders. Not surprisingly, they call their shop **(7) THE LAMPLIGHTER.** Daily 10-5. Closed Mon., or Tues. if Mon. is a holiday. 235-2306. VADA member.

"I try to start beginning collectors off right by telling them what to look for and what to avoid. Some sellers do terrible things to lamps." Alan Grace

"I knock on doors to get my pieces and I'll go anywhere. When residents discover that I'm honest, they tell their neighbors." Tony Costantino

Retrace your route, heading north on 133 about 5 miles. Bear right on Clarendon Springs Rd. to reach **(8) CLARENDON HOUSE, INC.**, in the former Clarendon Springs Hotel. Bonnie and Tony Costantino offer an ever-changing inventory of country and formal 19th-century furniture, paintings, rugs, folk art, toys, and vintage clothing. Not only are the Costantinos knowledgeable about their inventory, but they'll share with you the fascinating history of this former resort that was once the best-known mineral springs spa in Vermont. Visitors travelled north to take the cure. The hotel was built in 1834 to accommodate them, with sweeping porches and stately columns in the Southern tradition. Antiques fill a former country store and two floors of the hotel. Call ahead for your convenience and set aside plenty of time to

explore. You won't regret it. 438-2449. VADA member.

Continue on Rt. 133, then turn east on Rt. 4 to the business district of Rutland. Take a right on Court St., then a left on Center. At 90 Center St. Tom Conway has built an impressive reputation since he started **(9) CONWAY'S ANTIQUES** in 1956. You'll find an array of American, Chinese, and English furniture and specialty pieces like Rose Medallion and Imari porcelain, Oriental rugs, old prints, and paintings. Conway is also a talented interior designer and can advise you on setting up your new home or redecorating an old one. Mon.-Fri. 9:30-5, Sat. to noon. 775-5153. VADA member.

At the end of Center St. (about a half-block), you can get back on route 7 heading north. Drive 6 1/2 miles and look for a small sign on the left in front of **(10) MICHAEL AND LUCINDA SEWARD ANTIQUES**. (If you pass Jewett's Meats, you've over-shot your goal.) Michael sells mainly to other dealers and is known for Americana, such as silhouettes, weathervanes, painted boxes, early board games, and toys. Among his quality stock, culled from local homes and auctions, I wanted to buy several landscapes and prints by Vermont artists. His wife, Lucinda, showed me choice examples of yelloware, hooked rugs, pottery, and early quilts. Merchandise moves quickly here; what you see

"I like to educate people about antiques and encourage them to visit museums. A piece in its original state has real integrity and a fascinating story to tell us. The demand for such objects will always exceed the supply." Michael Seward

today may be gone tomorrow. They prefer serious buyers and suggest a phone call ahead. 483-6434. www.sover.net/~antinfo/ VADA member.

About a mile farther north on the right **(11) THE CRIMSON BUGGY** has long since collapsed, but the shop that takes its name carries on in the hands of its owners Barbara and John Schmidt. If musty smells bother your nose, skip this one. But there are some gems in this cluttered store if you're willing to take the time to poke around. I spotted lots of cut glass and Sterling silver, several stained-glass windows, jewelry in good condition, and toys. Daily 10-4. Closed Wed. 483-2804.

If you're intrigued by the history of New England (and didn't know that Vermont is the country's top maple syrup producer), consider a visit to the **(12) NEW ENGLAND MAPLE MUSEUM** about a mile farther north on the right. Its brochures call it "the sweetest story ever told." You'll not only learn the history of the sugaring process; you'll see a huge collection of sugaring artifacts as well as modern equipment. Daily 10-4. Closed January and February. 483-9414.

On route 7 in Brandon Center, **(13) NUTTING HOUSE ANTIQUES** is a group shop owned by Pamela and David Laubscher. Pam repairs hooked rugs and Dave answers your questions about the country furniture, folk art, and collectibles they carry. Among the items on display when I visited: a wood-carved hobby horse for $575, a decorated tool chest made in New Hampshire for $325, and a broad selection of baskets and hooked

"We've been in Brandon for 17 years and enjoy watching it grow. It's an up-and-coming destination for arts and antiques." David Laubscher

rugs. In the basement are shutters, doors, pedestals and more "as found," meaning, in this case, that they need repair. April-Dec. 31, Mon.-Sat. 10-5. 247-3302 or 800 870-9866.

Across the street, **(14) LEE B. PIRKEY** specializes in country pieces like pie safes, dry sinks, and slant-front desks. She insists that she tries to keep prices affordable, so if you're tempted, try to bargain. She sells daily from 10-5, off-season Fri.-Tues. 10-4. 247-3277.

(15) ANDREWS ANTIQUES is housed in a red barn, just off route 7 between Brandon and Middlebury on West Salisbury Rd. Jeff Andrews sells a mix of country pieces, like Adirondack chairs, and formal pieces, like a mahogany chest with ball-and-claw feet. I saw a Swiss music box sitting side by side an early American tin document box. Andrew's huge highway sign is all the advertising he says he needs to draw in customers. Daily. 352-6016.

Continue north on Rt. 7 until it intersects with Rt. 116. On the left is **(16) THE BARN**, an emporium of odd-ball items that will give you some laughs and not deflate your wallet. Wight Manning and Jim Blanchette have amassed FBI Most-Wanted posters, Coca Cola signs, mounted deer heads, wagon wheels, cookie jars, and more in five sprawling rooms. Need a gizmo? Just ask. 388-7584.

When you're ready for some serious buying, walk across the road to the **(17) MIDDLEBURY ANTIQUE CENTER, INC.** Francis Stevens and his wife Dianne bought this former bar and restaurant in 1987 and remodeled it to showcase the trophies of 54 dealers, about 40 of whom live in Vermont. You'll find Candy and Dan Tiley's toys and country furniture, Betty Ellovich's ceramics and small paintings, Dave and Jane Thompson's daguerrotypes,

"This is not a flea market. We try to stay away from collectibles, like Depression glass, or anything that's not at least 100 years old." Francis Stevens

Chris Waters' maps, and Lloyd Harrell's duck decoys and a pair of life-size, bronze black labs. If you prefer Americana, you can choose from Shaker boxes, Currier and Ives prints, jugs, blanket chests, and whirligigs, all priced to sell. Unlike many group shops, this center is well designed and staffed by professionals. Its extensive Website is also well-designed. Daily. 9-6. 388-6229. 800 339-6229. www.middantiques.com. VADA member.

Take a jog 2 miles north on route 116 until you spot **(18) BIX ANTIQUES** on the left. Laurie and John Wetmore maintain a varied selection of country and Victorian furniture in "as found" and refinished condition. They have space for huge tables and four-poster beds as well as cookbooks, china, woodenware, linens, and tools. Tues.-Sat. 9-5 Mar.-Dec. Closed Sun. Mon. by chance or appointment. 388-2277 or 800 486-4355.

Return to route 7 now and drive north 1 mile. **(19) DR. TOM'S ANTIQUES** refers to owner Tom Comes skills in "doctoring" ailing furniture. "Furniture cured from functional and appearance disorders" is what his business card promises. Repair and refinishing are his specialties, and he'll show you plenty of examples of his work in this two-story building. Country cupboards, blanket boxes, chests, and tables are all good bets. He gets his best pieces from local homes. Mon.-Sat. 9-5. Sun. by chance. 388-0153.

SIDE TRIPS

MIDDLEBURY. THE HENRY SHELDON MUSEUM preserves an 1829 marble merchant's mansion with no less than six marble mantelpieces. Rooms are furnished with period antiques, clothing, books, games, and other authentic artifacts. Guided tours, research collection, and changing exhibits. $4. 1 Park St. 388-2117. THE VERMONT FOLKLIFE CENTER is a great resource for history buffs, collecting Vermont traditional arts and folkways, such as storytelling, on tape and in its publications. A growing and important collection. 3 Court St. 388-4964.

PLACES TO STAY

WALLINGFORD: Innkeepers Tom and Jo Ann Brem welcome guests to the **I.B. MUNSON HOUSE** at 37 So. Main St. (route 7), an Italianate Victorian mansion. Each of seven guestrooms has a private bath; two feature fireplaces and claw-footed tubs. Breakfast and an afternoon snack included, dinner optional. If you really need quiet, this is a good choice. Nonsmoking. $55-$160. 446-2860 or 888-519-3771. www.ibmunsoninn.com.

BRANDON: A romantic getaway and luxurious overnight is the LILAC INN and restaurant at 53 Park St. You'll enjoy exploring this Greek Revival mansion and grounds with its spacious ballroom (popular for concerts and wedding receptions), library, dining room, patio, and gardens. $125-$195 off-season, $185-$260 foliage season and holidays. Includes breakfast. Tavern and dining room serve dinner Wed.-Sat. 247-5463 or 800 221-0720. www.lilacinn.com.

MIDDLEBURY: THE SWIFT HOUSE INN is in the village of Middlebury at 25 Stewart Lane. The elegant estate of a former Vermont governor, this mansion has fireplaces in bedrooms, double whirlpool tubs, a steam room and a sauna. $100-195. Dining room serves dinners 5:30-9. 388-9925. www.swifthouseinn.com.

PLACES TO EAT

BRANDON: SULLY'S PLACE is a friendly eatery on the main drag next to Nutting House Antiques. Bar on the left side, diningroom on the right, patio dining in front. Sunday brunch at 9. Lunch and dinner daily 11-9. 247-3223.

BRANDON INN. Guests enjoy lunch and dinner inside or on the terrace that overlooks the village green daily except Tues. and Wed.

Expect kitchen wizardry at moderate prices from chef-owner Louis Pattis. Children welcome. 247-5766 or 800 639-8685. www.brandoninn.com.

MIDDLEBURY: THE DOG TEAM TAVERN is 3 miles north of Middlebury off route 7 on Dog Team Rd. Started 50 years ago by doctor and missionary Sir Wilfred Grenfell and his wife Anne, the walls of this tavern are covered with the hooked rugs the couple sold to feed the poor in Labrador and Newfoundland. Its artwork and relics are the stuff of local legend. The dining experience is family style and favors New England dishes. Cocktail lounge. Dinner Mon.-Sat. 5-9, Sun. 12-9. 388-7651 or 800 472-7651. www.dogteamtavern.com.

ROLAND'S PLACE at the 1796 House is about 1/2 mile north of the Dog Team Tavern on route 7. Chef Roland Gaujac serves lunch, dinner, and Sunday brunch seven days a week in an inn built by one of the Green Mountain Boys. Sunday brunch is a la carte and includes everything from eggs Benedict to crab cakes; dinners range from $14-$19. 453-6309.

TRAVEL DIARY

TRAVEL DIARY

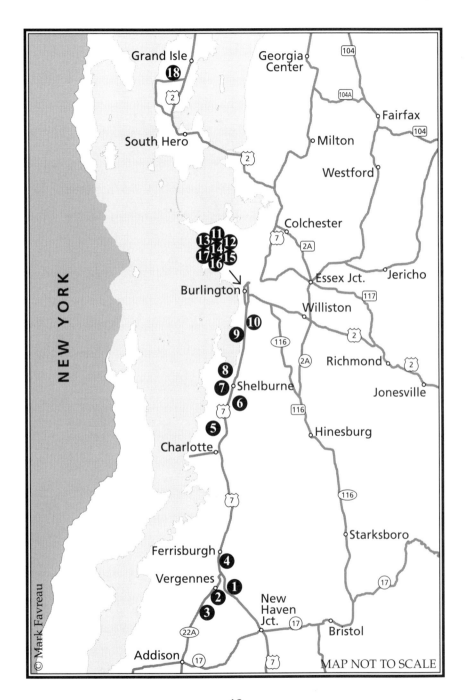

Itinerary 3

VERGENNES TO BURLINGTON
by route 7
Miles: 25

About 12 miles north of Middlebury and one mile south of Vergennes, you'll spot **(1) FITZ-GERALD'S** big gray house and red barn. Barbara and Joe Fitz-Gerald have amassed five of everything, except—they stress—glass, china, and dolls. Certainly no dolls, not next to the hunting knives, cannons, military gear, bear traps, and hand tools in the front room of their "masculine" shop. In the house, their stock is somewhat categorized: one room for clocks, another for country furniture, mostly from out-of-state; and bells, bells from trains, schools, sleighs, churches, farms, and yokes. But in the barn next door, it's strictly "furniture as found," which is great if you're looking to replace a window shutter or a porch column. When I last visited, Barbara

Fitz-Gerald's big gray house is a local landmark for antiquers with time to browse in Vergennes

had unearthed a key that fit a customer's 18th-century door. I had the feeling such miracles are common. Yearround Mon.-Sat. from 8 a.m. 877-2539.

Turn left at the sign for Vergennes and route 22A. The city of Vergennes is enjoying a cultural and commercial renaissance: two fine shops on Main St. (route 22A) are reason enough to visit. Washburn is Laura L. Sheidow's maiden name and this shop being her "maiden voyage," she named it **(2) WASHBURN ANTIQUES**. There is something for everyone here—country furniture, Bennington crocks, whirligigs, weathervanes, coverlets, and quilts. I admired a tall 1820 Maine clock, a partner's desk, and a harvest table, all nicely refinished. Daily. 877-1558.

"I wanted a shop that offered both new gifts and fine antiques. Apparently, the marriage worked. My customers are pleased."
Laura L. Sheidow

Mike Wilson of Stone Block Antiques

Walk down two blocks to 219 Main St., where Greg Hamilton and Mike Wilson co-own **(3) STONE BLOCK ANTIQUES.** Hamilton is expert in silverware and fishing tackle, Wilson in rare books. Together they have over 50 years of collecting experience, which they happily share with those just starting to collect. Wilson enjoys talking about antiques so much he organized a discussion group that meets in Brandon during the winter. You'll find a large range of items in this beautiful shop—canopy beds, gilt mirrors, Indian and farm baskets, china, and country furniture. Tues-Sat. 11-5. Sun. and Mon. by chance or appointment. 877-3359.

Follow 22A north until it meets route 7. Turn onto 7 and look for **(4) EIGHTH ELM FARM ANTIQUES** on your right. Paulette and Bob McNary offer a large selection of iron and brass beds and affordable country and Victorian furniture. They keep

"We've been in business 23 years and Vermonters know our reputation for quality refinishing. We repair, we don't rebuild, and we try to keep the furniture as authentic as possible." Bob McNary

refinished pieces in their home, "as found" pieces in the barn, and advertise good quality at fair prices. Fri.-Wed. 11-7. 877-3218.

(5) SHELBURNE MUSEUM is a collection of 37 historic buildings transplanted from all corners of New England to create a time capsule on 45 acres. You can walk through an apothecary shop with its herbs and patent medicines, blacksmith shop, covered bridge, general store, horseshoe barn, jail, meeting house, printing shop, sawmill, schoolhouse, round barn, 10-wheel steam locomotive, smokehouse, Shaker shed, sidewheel steamboat, and several furnished houses. The Stagecoach Inn displays founder Electra Havemeyer Webb's fascinating collection of folk art, such as ship's figureheads, trade signs, and her favorite—cigar store figures. There are exhibits from recent eras, such as the 1950s House, which recreates

post-World War II Vermont. Get a map at the visitors center and allow at least 4 hours if you want to see everything. But you can also pick and choose, hopping on and off the jitney along the one-mile route. Daily 10-5 late-May through late-October. $7-$17.50 admission. 985-3346. www.shelburnemuseum.org.

Opposite the museum, **(6) VINCENT J. FERNANDEZ** sells antiques and antique Oriental rugs from Persia, Turkey, India, Pakistan, China, and the Causcasus. 985-2275. VADA member. A

bit farther north on the left side of route 7, Deb Loveitt's **(7) SHELBURNE VILLAGE ANTIQUES** offers a complete line of New England country furniture and decorative pieces. She told me she tries to be very affordable to accommodate couples just starting to build a collection and has one-drawer stands from $225 and tables from $355. She also changes the shop according to the season; in the spring, I saw garden items, like gates, fountains, and planters. Unlike many dealers who sell by

"I find my best pieces in estate sales and family collections here in northern New England. I'm drawn to early American furniture, primitives, hooked rugs, and I have a special weakness for Windsor chairs." Deb Loveitt

appointment, Loveitt receives customers every day all year. 985-1447. VADA member.

Next door to Loveitt, George S. Colpitts has a fine collection of early American furniture, Chinese and Imari porcelain, Currier and Ives prints, Bennington stoneware, Sandwich glass, lots of burl bowls, and Staffordshire figures. I coveted a tiger maple sideboard and a 1780 Rhode Island chest the last time I visited. **(8) SOMERVILLE HOUSE ANTIQUES** is open Wed.-Sat. 10-5 and Sun 11:30-3:30 but Colpitts advises a phone call ahead in case he's at a show. 985-3431.

George S. Colpitts owns Somerville House Antiques

Collectors with a weakness for clocks will want to head to Gary LaPan's **(9) IT'S ABOUT TIME, LTD.**, about .5 mile north of Shelburne Village. A temporary detour around Route 7 takes you past his shop on Webster Road. Look for his sign on the left. LaPan stocks an intriguing selection of grandmother and grandfather clocks, schoolhouse clocks, calendar clocks, ship's chronometers, and a $1400 18-karat gold pocket watch I wanted to pocket myself. Each item carries a two-year warranty and LaPan makes repairs himself. Mon., Wed., and Fri. 10-6, Sat. 11-5. 985-5772.

Three miles north on Route 7, you can't miss the **(10) BURLINGTON CENTRE FOR ANTIQUES**. Just look for the handcarved brown bear holding a blue trout. With 80 dealers' wares displayed within 10,000 square feet, you might tell Manager Diana Vincent what priceless heirloom you're seeking and she can steer you in the right direction (which may be out the door). Furniture at the high end includes a tiger maple and cherry desk crafted by Asa Loomis of Shaftsbury circa 1815 and at the low end, oak dressers and stands. You'll see Lorette Sousie's linens, James Webb's clocks, and lots of pottery, china, and glass. Sun.-Thur. 10-5, Fri.-Sat. 10-6. 985-4911

"Our customers are very creative in adapting old pieces to modern uses. They will convert a doughbox to a planter, a commode to a night stand, a flat trunk to a coffee table, or a buffet to a bathroom vanity. People like to think they are getting a bargain, and we will always entertain a reasonable offer."
Diana Vincent

47

Follow route 7 into Burlington. Flynn Ave. is two traffic lights after the Shelburne Rd. Plaza on your left. Drive several blocks on Flynn Ave. to the railroad tracks. **(11) WHISTLE STOP ANTIQUES** and **(12) UPSTAIRS ANTIQUES** face each other in renovated warehouses. Jeanne Shea owns Whistle Stop, a group shop new as of September 1999. Shea has room to spare for her dealers, whose inventory runs mostly to smalls, collectibles, and used furniture. Daily 10-5. 951-9189.

Upstairs Antiques is the creation of David Robbins and if you love 1950s nostalgia, you've come to the right place. He admitted to me that part of his pleasure is listening to customers' hilarious reactions to a dachsund-shaped cheese server, a deer-hoof thermostat, cow key-holders, wrought-iron swag ceiling lamps, a Titanic life-preserver made of cement, and a 3-foot-high cocktail shaker. Apart from gag gifts, Robbins has a nice collection of doll house furniture, toy soldiers, and cigar molds. Welcome to the funhouse, especially if Robbins is your tour guide. Daily. 859-8966.

> **"Bad stuff is good. I try to find things that are well made, stylish, and fun. They are not strictly antiques, but they do appeal to the imagination."**
> **David Robbins**

Retrace your route to Pine St., turn left and just past Howard St. is **(13) THE LAMP SHOP.** Liz Segal and Andy Arp sell various vintage lighting—such as chandeliers, pendant lights, and sconces—as well as glass and fabric shades. They'll also repair an antique lamp you might have purchased that needs to be rewired or has a frayed cord. www.thelampshopvt.com. 864-6782. A few doors down at 270 Pine St. is **(14) CONANT CUSTOM BRASS**, perhaps the premier site in New England for antique lighting. They have over 300 restored light fixtures and hundreds of glass shades in stock as well as antiques in copper and brass, like andirons and mantel clocks. 8:30-6 Mon.-Fri., 10-5 Sat. 658-4482 or 800 832-4482. www.conantcustombrass.com.

Continue down Pine St. and turn left on Main to find the **(15) ARCHITECTURAL SALVAGE WAREHOUSE**. David Ackerman has rescued an amazing variety of stained glass, fireplace mantels, pillars, early hardware, clawfoot bathtubs, French doors, marble sinks, and other discarded treasures. This is a goldmine to couples restoring an older home. You can preview his current selections by browsing his excellent Website. Mon.-Sat. 10-5. 658-5011. www.architecturalsalvagevt.com.

At 31-35 Main St., Deborah Barnum sells about 3,000 antiquarian books among the oldies but goodies on her shelves. **(16) BYGONE BOOKS** will please bibliophiles as well as those in search of a good read. Daily. 862-4397. **(17) NORTH COUNTRY BOOKS**, on the other hand, sells only collectible and rare books, as well as maps, prints, and LP records. To find this shop, head east on Main St., turn left on Church, and near the intersection with Pearl look for Banana Republic. The bookstore is ensconced beneath Banana Republic at 2 Church St. Mon.-Thur. 9:30-7, Fri.-Sat. 9:30-9, Sun. 11-6. 862-6413.

SIDETRIPS

(18) VALLEE'S DEN OF ANTIQUITY in Grand Isle on Rt. 2 is 23 miles north of Burlington. An experience not limited to shopping with Professor René Valle, author of *Tales of a Vermont Antiques Trader.* Old and new are mixed, but each item is marked as to age and origin. Glass, decoys, primitives, Victoriana, Arts and Crafts, an art gallery, and library each have their separate spaces; furniture is displayed throughout the 9,000 square feet of this 1810 English cow barn. No reproductions, including the Rolls Royce parked in the driveway. If you can't find it here, you haven't looked. May-Nov. daily 11-5:30. 372-8324.

WILSON'S CASTLE is an architectural marvel about 8 miles off route 7 in Proctor. The castle's 32 rooms boast 84 stained-glass windows, 13 fireplaces, European and Far Eastern furnishings, and an art gallery. Tours depart daily 9-5:30 late May through mid-Oct. $7. 773-3284.

ROKEBY MUSEUM, 3 miles north of Vergennes in Ferrisburgh, preserves the history of four generations of a Quaker family, one of whose members was 19th-century author, illustrator, and naturalist Rowland E. Robinson. On route 7. $4. Guided tours from Thur.-Sun. May though Oct. and by appointment at other times. 877-3406

PLACES TO STAY

BURLINGTON. THE WILLARD STREET INN at 349 South Willard St. near the University of Vermont campus. Breakfast in this Queen Anne-style mansion is served in the solarium, a bright space with marble-tiled floors and white-beamed ceiling. Views of Lake Champlain. Fourteen spacious rooms are priced from $115-$225. Nonsmoking. Guests get 20 percent off their meals at Isabel's on the Waterfront restaurant. 651-8710 or 800 577-8712. www.willardstreetinn.com.

SHELBURNE. THE INN AT SHELBURNE FARMS is 2 miles west of route 7 on Harbor Rd. Open May 15-Oct. 15. Rooms vary in size and price from $100-$350 depending on the season. Two cottages. This is a restored 1899 mansion on the spacious grounds of a working farm. Start your Christmas shopping early by stocking up on their hams, cheeses, and syrup. Breakfast and dinner are served in an elegant dining room. 985-8498. www.shelburnefarms.org.
HEART OF THE VILLAGE INN. Walk to the Shelburne Museum from your room in this Queen Anne-style B&B. Nine rooms have private baths, telephones, and AC. $95-$200. 985-2800 or 877-808-1834. www.heartofthevillage.com.

PLACES TO EAT

VERGENNES. Christophe's on the Green, at the corner of Main and Green Streets, is named for chef-owner Christophe Lissarrague. He prepares mouthwatering French country dishes and has an efficient billing system. Appetizers: $9.50, dinner entrees: $24.50, desserts and cheeses: $9, prix fixe dinner: $38. No parties larger than 8. Reservations recommended. Tues.-Sat. 5:30-9:30 May 14-Oct.21. 877-3413.

SHELBURNE. The Inn at Shelburne Farms (see above). Dinners range from $19-$29.

SOUTH BURLINGTON. Pauline's Cafe and Restaurant at 1834 Shelburne Rd. Cafe offers lunch and light dinners in a casual atmosphere, full dinners upstairs. Homemade breads and desserts, organic produce, and regional specialties. Early dinner specials for $10.95 are a bargain. 862-108 or 800-491-1281.

BURLINGTON. Five Spice Cafe at 175 Church St. borrows from many culinary traditions—Chinese, Vietnamese, Thai, and Indian—to create its Asian feasts. My favorite? Evil Jungle Prince with Chicken followed by Ginger Tangerine Cheesecake. Lunch and dinner daily. Sunday dim sum brunch. 864-4045.

TRAVEL DIARY

TRAVEL DIARY

TRAVEL DIARY

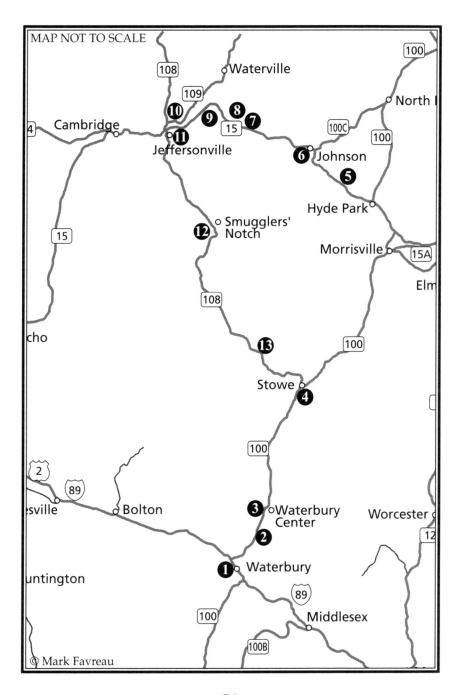

MAP NOT TO SCALE

100

108

○ Waterville

109

○ North

4   Cambridge

⑩

⑨

⑧

⑦

15

100C

100

⑪

Jeffersonville

⑥

○ Johnson

15

⑤

Hyde Park ○

○ Smugglers'
Notch

⑫

Morrisville ○

15A

Elm

108

⑬

100

Stowe ○

④

100

2

89

sville ○

○ Bolton

③

○ Waterbury
Center

Worcester

cho

12

②

untington

①

○ Waterbury

89

100

○ Middlesex

100B

© Mark Favreau

56

ITINERARY 4

WATERBURY TO STOWE
by routes 100, 15, and 108
Miles: 56

This scenic loop takes you from the busy Stowe intersection north through lazy pastureland in the Lamoille River Valley, up Mt. Mansfield and Smuggler's Notch State Park, descending on the return again to Stowe. Mt. Mansfield is the state's tallest peak and the outline of the mountain looks so much like a face that locals refer to its "forehead," "nose," "chin," and "Adam's apple." Once you're at the top of Mt. Mansfield, you can hike out to The Chin and view the countryside from a height of 4,393 feet.

Smuggler's Notch is actually a gap between Mt. Mansfield and Sterling Peak that's closed to car traffic in winter. It gets its name from independent Vermonters who defied the 1807 embargo against trading with Canada and Great Britain. They smuggled goods (and later slaves) to the north through this mountain passage.

Take exit 10 off I-89. Waterbury hosts one of the state's largest flea markets near this intersection. You can't miss it if you travel on a weekend from early May through early October. Call 244-7475 to check dates. Follow route 100 south into Waterbury village, turn left on Main St. and **(1) MARTHA LEWIS ANTIQUES** is on the corner of Main and Stowe. Lewis says she likes to stock "a little of everything." But popular items include her doll furniture, dishes, and other children's toys; 1950s nostalgia; and cran-

berry glass. She also carries a lot of china, silver, linens, and smalls, like salt sellers and butter dishes. Mon.-Sat. 10-5, Sun. 11-4. 244-8919.

A mile north of Waterbury on the right, across from Ben and Jerry's, is **(2) EARLY VERMONT ANTIQUES**. Barbara Parker has a mix of farm equipment outside and jewelry, smalls, collectibles, and some furniture inside. Daily 10-5. 244-5373. Two miles farn on the left is **(3) SIR RICHARD'S ANTIQUE CENTER,** ildings full of antiques and newer items. It saves time to , Richard and Barbara Woodward know what you're . You don't want to try to navigate this labyrinth with-

too . The Woodwards have been directing traffic in these ce 1971, and they're good at it. Cases of rare books, some not so rare, are clearly labelled. Fiestaware, Depression glass, and all manner of furniture are here. Make an offer and be sure to put a nickel in the slot machine on the counter before you leave. Hey, you never know. Daily 10-5. 244-8879. VADA member.

In Stowe, **(4) STOWE ANTIQUES CENTER** is on the right just past Mac's Market. Fred Paulette has a choice collection of both antique furniture and 18th-century reproductions by D.R. Dimes, early baskets, silver, paintings, folk art, and glassware. Daily 10-5. 253-9875 or 888-802-5441. www.stoweantiques.com

---

"There are signs that you look for when you're evaluating the age of a piece. Honest wear is hard to disguise, but you'd be surprised how many people try. I get taken every now and then." Fred Paulette

---

Continue north on Rt. 100 till it intersects with Rt. 15. Take Rt. 15 west about 4 miles and watch for **(5) KITTELL'S** faded red barns on the right. Arthur Kittell likes to buy and sell anything that's farm related, particularly early wrought iron. You'll see lots of lamps, both kerosene and electric, in his shop and furniture that he's refinished above it. "Assorted junk" is stored in a separate

59

barn. Expect the unexpected—like a pet raccoon. Daily. 635-7119.

At 325 Lower Main Street in the village of Johnson, Gordon and Janice Goodwin run **(6) VICTORIAN HOUSE ANTIQUES**, a group shop with 13 dealers. You'll find an array of country furniture, baskets, militaria, dolls, linens, books, and quilts. My favorite collectible was a Mickey Mouse cookie jar with those unmistakeable ears. Daily 9:30-5. 635-9549.

Just west of Johnson on the right side of route 15, **(7) MEL SIEGEL** has a deservedly fine reputation for country antiques and primitives, Majolica, mocha, Quimper, Staffordshire, flow blue, and farm tools. I saw plenty of blanket chests, cupboards, and tables in fine condition. Siegel's been a dealer since 1959, and if he doesn't have what you need, he can tell you where to get it. May-Oct. daily 9:30-5. 635-2000. VADA member.

"What customers see in my shop is what pleases me. I could fill up my shop with saleable items, but I prefer to buy what I love."
Mel Siegel

Next to Siegel is **(8) THE BUGGY MAN II**, an annex to the original shop a bit farther down the road. Owner Ed Barnes restored and decorated the Thomas McConnell House (1790) to show-off its unusual architecture. The result is a visually stunning space for period and formal furniture that's pricey but not inflat-ed. Some, like a New Hampshire highboy made about 1760, deserve to be in a museum. 635-7664.

The original **(9) BUGGY MAN ANTIQUES CENTER,** across route 15 with the carriages in front, grew from a vegetable stand 60 years ago. Barnes advertises "farmhouse antiques at country prices." Many have been restored so be sure to ask what parts have been replaced. Refinishing is generally high quality. Don't believe the "creative" descriptions of a piece's origins; they tend to

be far-fetched. In a shed that stored farm equipment, I saw a bright red cabriolet sleigh with blue velvet cushions that cried out for TLC. If you're fur-nishing a second home or just enjoy country furniture, plan to spend some time here. (Barnes and buddies insist that the real antiques maven is Cyrus McGillicuddy, their English springer spaniel. In fact, after listening to their jokes, I felt a little buggy

"We buy estates, and we run the gamut—everything from primitives to '50s kitsch. And I love it all."
Ed Barnes (with Cyrus McGillicuddy)

myself.) Daily 9-5. 635-2110.

Continue west towards Jeffersonville where Dick and Carolyn Hover run a group shop of 40 dealers in a converted barn they call **(10) 1829 HOUSE ANTIQUES.** Lots to browse here on three floors so plan accordingly. Mon.-Sat. 9-5. 644-2912. Turn south on route 108, where it intersects with route 15 and you'll be on Main St. in Jeffersonville. On the right you'll see an antiques sign. It points to **(11) VILLAGE BARN ANTIQUES,** which sits behind Jefferson House B&B. Richard and Joan Walker have a small, but interesting, selection of collectibles, like early game boards, country pieces, and children's toys. Daily. 644-2030.

(12) SMUGGLER'S NOTCH ANTIQUE CENTER is a mile south, next to Mannsview Inn. Kelley and Bette Mann, who own both places, augment their own inventory with that of 12 dealers

Kelley Mann co-owns Smuggler's Notch Antique Center

in a restored dairy barn. The Guernseys are gone, replaced by a country store at the front of the shop that sells candy, candles, and, of course, maple syrup. On two floors, Kelley displays furniture that's about 75 percent old, 25 percent new. He does a lot of custom work, converting sleighs into coffee tables, shingles into benches. He showed me several gorgeous new pieces in tiger maple. But I was more intrigued by a desk removed from the St. Albans Railroad Depot, made in the 1850s in oak and butternut. He likes to buy trade signs and the bigger the better. May-Oct. daily 10-5; Nov.-Apr. Sat.-Sun. 10-5. 644-8321.

Drive carefully through Smuggler's Notch State Park, always watching for bikers along this narrow route that winds through the gap between Mt. Mansfield and Sterling Peak. As you descend into the valley, about 10 miles from Jeffersonville, look for **(13) ROSEBUD ANTIQUES AT HOUSTON FARM** on the left. Ed and Jean Baldassare run a charming shop in back of their home that specializes in sports equipment and sports-related prints. You'll find vintage skis, snowshoes, sleighs and bells, and Adirondack pack baskets. They also have some top quality quilts and country furniture. Wed.-Sun. 10-5, Mon.-Tues. by chance or appointment. 253-2333.

"We collect antiques related to regional activities, like skiing and hiking. Vermont is also known for its chocolates and ice cream, so we have a collection of antique chocolate and ice cream molds."
Ed Baldassare

PLACES TO STAY

WATERBURY CENTER. THATCHER BROOK INN is just north of exit 10 on route 100. Named for the creek that runs nearby, this restored Victorian mansion offers Laura Ashley-decorated rooms with antiques, fireplaces, and whirlpool baths as well as a tavern and dining room. Nonsmoking. $80-$195. 244-5911 or 800-292-5911. www.thatcherbrook.com.

JEFFERSONVILLE. Joan and Dick Walker are your hosts at THE JEFFERSON HOUSE, a Victorian treasure with 3 bedrooms, a wraparound porch and cozy common rooms. Full breakfast. $55-$75. 644-2030 or 800-253-9630. 71 Main St. www.scenesofvermont.com/jeffhse/index.html.

SMUGGLER'S NOTCH. THE MANNSVIEW INN is next to Smuggler's Notch Antiques Center on route 108 south. Seven guestrooms in this restored colonial at the foot of Mt. Mansfield feature queensize poster beds with handmade quilts. Hot breakfast includes choice of omelette, waffles, blueberry pancakes or eggs Benedict. Library, billiard room, hot tub, and you can rent a canoe next door. Discounts to antiques dealers. $65-$125. 644-8321 or 888-937-6266. www.mannsview.com.

PLACES TO EAT

STOWE. FOXFIRE INN and Italian Restaurant. 1 1/2 miles north of Stowe on Route 100. Fine dining in a restored farmhouse. Eggplant Parmigiana and Chicken Repieno are specialties of chef Bob Manley, whose dinner entrees range from $12-$20. Daily 5:30-9:30. Reservations recommended. 253-4887.

GREEN MOUNTAIN INN has the casual Whip Bar and Grill, named for its collection of antique buggy whips, where chef Steve Truso serves lunch, dinner, and Sunday brunch. Dinner specials are listed on a blackboard menu and average $16.95. Daily 11:30-9:30. Also, the Main Street Dining Room serves breakfast. 253-7301 or 800-253-7302.

JOHNSON. Pat Persico commands the grill at PERSICO'S PLUM & MAIN for breakfast, lunch and dinner. Omelets are memorable, the soups homemade, and for dinner you can bring your own wine. Moderate prices. Weekdays 6 am-8 pm, Fri. and Sat. till 9, Sun. 8 am-1 pm. Main St. 635-7596.

TRAVEL DIARY

TRAVEL DIARY

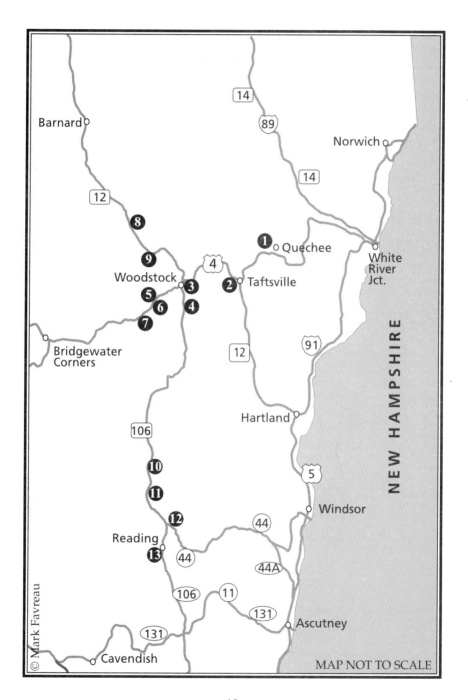

Barnard

⑭ 14

89

Norwich

14

⑫ 12

❽

❶ Quechee

White River Jct.

❾

4

Woodstock ❸
❺
❻
❹ ❷ Taftsville

❼

Bridgewater Corners

12

91

NEW HAMPSHIRE

Hartland

106

5

❿

⓫

Windsor

⓬

44

Reading
⓭

44

44A

106

11

131

Ascutney

131

Cavendish

© Mark Favreau

MAP NOT TO SCALE

ITINERARY 5

QUECHEE TO READING
by routes 4, 12, and 106
Miles: 23

Woodstock is a busy resort town and a mecca for antiques hunters. Its impressive architectural heritage is well preserved in the churches and fine Federal homes that encircle the village green. Not far from the green is a covered bridge for pedestrians only. Unlike itinerary #4, this tour demands very little driving because most shops are located in and around the village. The tour starts in Quechee, which is just east of Woodstock, on route 4. If you are approaching from the east, take exit 1 off I-89 and drive west on route 4 to the yellow blinking light. **(1) ANTIQUES COLLABORATIVE** is on your right.

You'll need at least an hour to browse the wares of over 150 dealers that Bill and Isabelle Bradley have assembled on three

**"One of the challenges for group-shop owners like us is quality control. We avoid renting our space just to fill it, and that sets us apart from other group shops in this area."
Bill Bradley**

floors in two restored buildings connected by a glass atrium. Don Slater's Irish country furniture is here as are Wayne Ridley's oriental rugs, Fred and Robin Little's jewelry, and Marie Miller's quilts, not to mention rare books, paintings and lithographs, silver, English porcelains, Lalique and Tiffany glass, Civil War memorabilia, and Native American artifacts. Unusual furniture includes two Eastlake pieces—a ladies desk and a cherry tree/bench for the hall. Expect new inventory every month and detailed labeling as to age and condition. 296-5858. Daily 10-5. VADA member

Continue on route 4 about 1 1/2 miles. You'll see the Taftsville Country Store on your left. (This upscale convenience store stocks everything from wines to imported cheeses and has a Post Office

"When we first started in business 37 years ago, we named our shop Heritage House. Soon everyone was copying us— fertilizer companies, breadmakers. So now we use our own name." Mary Fraser

in the back. If you need a snack and the *New York Times*, stop in.) Turn left on Happy Valley Rd. to reach **(2) FRASER'S ANTIQUES**, where Bob and Mary Fraser sell a variety of early Americana in their 1840 barn. Some of my favorites included an Abernaki Indian basket and 19th-century high-button shoes. Hooked rugs, coverlets, and blanket chests are always good bets here. The Frasers specialize in Vermont coin silver, such as Brinsmaid's, and are happy to dip into their collection of reference books on antiques to answer customers' questions. They also sell many books on collecting. By chance or appointment. 457-3437.

As you enter the village of Woodstock, watch for **(3) POLO ANTIQUES** on your left. The shop is named for owner Steve Leninski's favorite sport (if he's not there, he's probably on a horse). He's known for very early Americana and for his taste in choosing 18th- and 19th-century furniture, china, pewter, clocks, paintings, and prints. They are all displayed in this small house at 53 Pleasant St. Leninski's been a dealer for 45 years, formerly in Guilford, CT. Thur.-Mon. 10-5. 457-5837.

Next to Polo is **(4) PRAXIS**, which owner Peter Saman tells me means "harmony between what you're aware of and what you're doing." As you enter his shop, look for his logo on a wooden carved relief. He showed me fine examples of Vermont country furniture, including a station master's desk, chimney and jelly cupboards; painted and unpainted tables; chests; blanket boxes, and stands. Summer: 9-5, Winter: weekends and by chance. 457-2396. A bit farther down Pleasant St. on the right is **(5) PLEA-SANT STREET BOOKS** with over 10,000 antiquarian books in all fields. This shop is open summer and fall daily from 11-5, winter and spring Thur.-Sun. 11-5. 457-4050. VABA member.

(6) WIGREN-BARLOW'S white gravel parking lot sets the tone for this elegant shop at 29 Pleasant Street as do its fountains, flower gardens, and walk-through courtyard. This is one of Woodstock's oldest shops, doing business since 1959, and it specializes in garden ornaments—like urns, arches, gates, fountains—and architectural pieces. Spacious rooms house spacious furniture of French, American, and English provenance. I saw an 8-foot-long store counter, a 7-foot-long workbench, and a 6-foot-long Welsh dresser. My favorite? A three-foot-high mortar carved from a beech tree with a birch pestle. Furniture can be pricey, but manager Eric Nesbitt sells plenty of smalls priced as low as $20. Mon.-Sat. 10-5, Sun. 10-3. 457-2453. VADA member.

"We go in for gutsy pieces. Cupboards, hog benches, apothecary chests, sofas, and farm tables."
Eric Nesbitt

A block west at 71 Central St. is **(7) AMERICAN CLASSICS,** where Meryl and Jay Weiss proudly display their collection of quality Americana. In a bright and airy second floor space, Meryl showed me painted furniture—such as a New York chest and country kas circa 1820—and lots of hooked and braided rugs starting at $275. Great examples of folk art include a birch bark decorated canoe made by the Canadian Manouani tribe, a shooting gallery iron ram complete with bullet holes, and a canvas elephant from Ringling Bros. Barnum and Bailey circus. When I admired some tall, cane-woven baskets, Meryl explained that they were traps for catching eels but could be adapted to hold dried flowers. She has a gift for seeing the artistic potential in almost any object. Thur.-Tues. 10-5:30. 457-4337. VADA member.

"My customers are more eager for decorative art than they are for furniture. They buy antique signs and rugs and hang them on their walls." Meryl Weiss

---

One mile north of Woodstock on route 12 (which is also Elm St.) is another beautiful gallery in a modern building full of light.

(8) OLD DOG ANTIQUES is named for Robin Fernsell's favorite pet, Jeeter. It's located at the apex where route 12 intersects Pomfret Road. Like American Classics, Robin has the space to display large pieces of Americana, like a six-foot-high rocking horse, dartboards, vibrant rugs, and weathervanes. She has an impressive selection of 18th- and 19th-century country pieces in their original paint and old finish, folk art, primitives, paintings, hooked rugs, and Shaker pieces. The one I coveted was a watercolor fraktur of Adam, Eve, and the Serpent. Folk art here is steep, but most pieces are one-of-a-kind. Daily by chance or appointment. 457-9800. VADA member.

On your way back to Woodstock, **(9) BILLINGS FARM AND MUSEUM** might be your next stop if you've an interest in the fast-disappearing Vermont farm life. You can tour a working dairy farm, livestock barns, and a restored farmhouse here. The museum offers exhibits of Vermont's rural past and the 1999 documentary "A Place in the Land." May-October 10-5. Daily. 457-2355. www.billingsfarm.org.

When you reach Woodstock, head south on 106. Exactly 10 miles south, look for a sign on the left just beyond Whitmore Circle. James and Elizabeth Harley's **(10) YELLOW HOUSE ANTIQUES** sits back from the road and is easy to miss. They specialize in Shaker pieces of museum quality, such as a tall cupboard and many fine chairs from the New Lebanon, NY, Shaker community. Toleware document boxes circa 1830 range from $350 to $450, and I was particularly drawn to a hearth rug hooked in homespun wool with brilliant red flowers bordered by scallop shells. The Harley's are especially proud of a calimanco quilt c.1790 that belonged to the family of Civil War general George McClellan. It's glazed with gum arabic to highlight its intricate quilting. By chance or appointment. 484-7799. VADA member. www.antweb.com/yellowhouse.

Farther south on 106, John and Nancy Stahura use their barn to showcase early American furniture, primitives, stoneware, silver, baskets, and quilts at **(11) MILL BROOK ANTIQUES**. I spotted an 1800s butter churn in original red paint, several early samplers in good condition, Windsor chairs, crocks, mirrors, and a sweet collection of chocolate molds. John and Nancy are particularly knowledgeable about early American furniture and folk art. I asked John what he looked for when he was dating a piece of furniture. "Rosehead nails date a piece to the early 1800s. Craftsmen in those days had the time to make fine cuts and to do dovetailing and beading. Planing marks and saw cuts indicate age as well as the size of boards. We don't have the two-foot-wide boards they had 100 years ago. You'll notice that collectors and dealers always look at the back and bottom of a piece rather than the front. They might pull out the drawer of a chest, for example, and feel for champhoring (cuts around the sides). Craftsmanship and wear are hard to disguise." Daily. 484-5942. VADA member.

Next on the left after Mill Brook Antiques is **(12) LIBERTY HILL ANTIQUES**, where Jim and Suzan Mulder have a small selection of original and refinished country pieces and a wide selection of woodworking tools, such as a cooper's plane circa 1858 used to make barrels. May-Oct. Daily. Off-season by appointment. 484-7710. VADA member.

One mile south of Reading, look for the buggy that announces

(13) BLACK HORSE FARM on the right. Holly Martin offers a selection of cupboards and other country pieces, plus folk art painted on antique boxes and trunks, and handmade Nantucket Lightship baskets she calls Vertuckets. Daily, but not summer 2000, or by appointment. 484-3539.

SIDETRIPS

Two historical museums are worth a peek, if time permits. **THE WOODSTOCK HISTORICAL SOCIETY** at 26 Elm St (route 12) exhibits 1740-1900 furniture, paintings, decorative pieces, toys, tools, and more in the 1807 Dana House. Tours start on the hour Mon.-Sat. 10-5, Sun. noon-4. $1. 457-1822. **THE DAUGHTERS OF THE AMERICAN REVOLUTION HOUSE AND MUSEUM** offers an interesting local collection at 22 The Village Green.

PLACES TO STAY

QUECHEE. THE QUECHEE INN at MARSHLAND FARM. A real country exierence in this 1793 inn with 24 guestrooms. You can hike trails, fly fish, canoe, and cross-country ski when you're not enjoying gourmet meals prepared by Kirk Jones. $100-$220 for B&B or $140-$260 for MAP. Quechee Main St. 295-3133 or 800-235-3133. www.quecheeinn.com.

WOODSTOCK. THREE CHURCH STREET is the address of an antique-filled Georgian mansion surrounded by lawn and gardens. Innkeeper Eleanor Paine offers 11 guest rooms, a full breakfast, and swimming and tennis in summer. $75-$115 . Near the green. 457-1925.

SOUTH WOODSTOCK. KEDRON VALLEY INN. Innkeepers Max and Merrily Comins have created one of the most relaxing hideaways in the state with a prize-winning menu and wine list. Their 60-piece quilt collection graces the walls and guestrooms. Most rooms have canopy beds, several have fireplaces, decks or terraces, and jacuzzis. $131-$297 includes breakfast. Pond swimming, hiking, and horseback riding nearby. Route 106, 5 miles south of Woodstock. 457-1473 or 800 836-1193. www.innformation.com/vt/kedron.

PLACES TO EAT

QUECHEE. SIMON PEARCE RESTAURANT. In an old mill on the Ottauquechee River you can watch handblown glass and pottery being created and then buy them—as well as linens, woolen goods, and leather—in retail shops. Dine overlooking a waterfall and covered bridge. Lunch 11:30-2:45; dinner 6-9. Dinner entrees cost $16-$25, reservations are recommended. 295-1470. www.simonpearceglass.com

WOODSTOCK. MOUNTAIN CREAMERY serves hearty breakfasts and soup, sandwiches, and daily specials from 7-6. A pastry and espresso shop downstairs satisfies your sweet tooth with hand-made ice cream, candies, and assorted goodies. 33 Central St. in the heart of the village. 457-1715.

SOUTH WOODSTOCK. KEDRON VALLEY INN. Chef Jim Allen's mouthwatering dinner menu includes his specialty, Maine salmon stuffed with seafood mousse and wrapped in puff pastry, as well as baked sea scallops on a bed of sliced artichoke hearts and shi-take mushrooms. Fresh veggies really have pizzazz. House guests pay a fixed price of $35 for a 5-course meal. The public can order a la carte entrees that range from $17-26. (See above).

TRAVEL DIARY

TRAVEL DIARY

TRAVEL DIARY

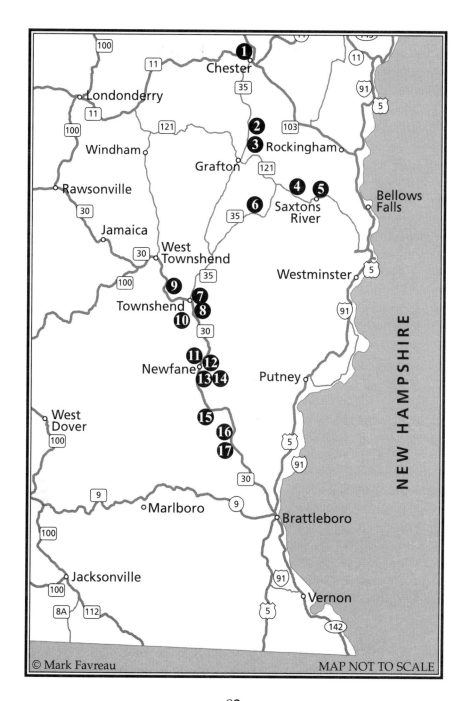

ITINERARY 6

CHESTER TO SOUTH NEWFANE
by routes 35, 121, and 30
Miles: 42

This is an unhurried tour over secondary roads with none of the heavy traffic that clogs major arteries like Manchester, Burlington, Stowe, and Woodstock. Once out of bustling Chester, the route winds through country villages like Grafton and Newfane that many consider to be the essence of New England.

Start your tour in Chester, notable for its pre-Civil War stone houses, whistlestops on the Underground Railroad. Where routes 11 west and 103 north converge at 42 Maple St., you'll spot the sign for **(1) WILLIAM AUSTIN'S ANTIQUES.** It decorates the lawn of a white clapboard house with green and gold trim. Shopping here can be overwhelming, unless you're trying to fill a 22-room house. Owner Bill Smith claims to have over 300 pieces of country and formal furniture in this emporium, and that includes every-thing from Hoosier cabinets to oak ice boxes. Some antiques have been adapted to modern uses, like sleigh coffee tables. Lots of bed-room and diningroom sets. Daily 9-6, Fri. till 9. Closed Easter, Thanksgiving, and Christmas. 875-3032 or 877 447-5268.

Now head south on route 35. This is a twisty, turny road through woodland, very refreshing on a hot day and a riot of color in autumn. After 4 miles turn left on Eastman Rd. (which is unpaved) and watch for the "Antiques" sign on the right that directs you to Mary and Peter Pill's **(2) GRAFTON GATHERING PLACE**. This is one of the most outstanding collections of pre-

Mary and Peter Pill of Grafton Gathering Place

1840s antiques in the state, so take time to admire their early period and high-style country pieces. Like the Stahuras, Peter and Mary are generous with their time and know-how. "I think most dealers," Peter told me, "look for hard-to-find items, such as whimsies. Most whimsies had no particular use and were made from leftover materials." As an example of such Yankee inventiveness, he showed me a pitcher made out of sewer tile. Peter also pointed to a portrait of a wizened old woman. "Notice anything odd about her glasses?" he asked. "The spokes are outside her bonnet," I answered. "It's a posthumous painting," he explains. "Itinerant artists trying to build a business painted the deceased as if she were still alive, but the glasses give it away as well as the Forget-me-not she's holding in her hand." Daily 10-5. Closed Tues. except during foliage season. 875-2309. VADA member

About a mile farther along Eastman Rd., turn left on Illingsworth Rd. and follow it up the hill bearing left at the sign for **(3) SYLVAN HILL ANTIQUES.** Thelma and Albin Zak's shop is named for its setting and panoramic mountain views. Their collection of American and English period furniture and decorative art is no less impressive: it yields such treasures as a 1775 Philadephia desk, an oak child's coffer made in England about 1680, and an English cutlery box. Thelma likes to buy children's antiques, such as cradles and highchairs; Mason ironstone china; brass and copper; treenware (plates, bowls, and spoons made from trees); and the American and English samplers and paintings that decorate her walls. Daily 10-5 by chance or appointment. 875-3954. VADA member.

"I specialize in English high-country period furniture. That's what I am known for. But I'll always take a special piece of American furniture if it fits the look of my shop." Thelma Zak

Retrace your route back to route 35 and head south. Grafton is a timeless hamlet, like Brigadoon, thanks to the generosity and savvy planning of the Windham Foundation. Beginning in 1963, this nonprofit corporation bought and resurrected 50 buildings, including the inn, general store, blacksmith shop, and cheese factory. The result? Grafton's tiny population of 600 is augmented by a steady stream of visitors, especially leaf-peepers. Stop for lunch at the Old Tavern and take a peek at one of Vermont's oldest inns, built in 1801. Or visit any one of three museums, hike marked footpaths in summer or crosscountry ski the same paths in winter.

When you're ready to retake the road, follow route 121 east exactly 4.8 miles and turn at the blue mailbox and sign for **(4) SCHOOLHOUSE ANTIQUES.** Faith Boone and Sandy Saunders have two floors of country furniture, both painted and refinished, in an addition to their ranch house. Accessories include hooked and braided rugs, samplers and silhouettes, mirrors, ironwork, and woodenware. No china, silver, or glass. They've been in business since 1972 and buy most of their wares from other dealers or private homes. Call ahead or you might miss them. Yearround. 869-2332. VADA member.

Another 2.2 miles east brings you to the village of Saxtons River and the **(5) SIGN OF THE RAVEN** on Main Street. And what the raven quoth (at least in words at the shop's entrance) is:

86

Entrance to the Sign of the Raven in Saxtons River

"A Reprieve from Mediocrity." That's Bob and Mary Ellen Warner's description for the barn full of early American treasures well arranged on two floors. They've been dealing for 32 years and are happy to share their tips on building a collection and spotting a "fake." There are lots of tables of glass, silver, and china as well as furniture in its original paint, pewter, rugs, paintings, and Oriental pieces, some priced as low as $25. May-Nov daily. 869-2500. VADA member.

Retrace your route until route 121 intersects with 35. A few miles south on route 35 stop in at **(6) ATHENS ANTIQUE PRINTS AND THE RICHTER GALLERY.** Allison Richter and Stephen Zeigfinger's shop is an extraordinary homage to antique advertising and vintage prints. You'll see embossed cigar boxes and their beautifully detailed labels, seed packs, catalogs, signs, and candy boxes. Their collection of antique prints includes maps, handcolored botanicals, and Art Deco. All their conservation matting and framing is done on the premises. Daily 869-2722. www.sover.net/~oldlabel.

"There was just one way to advertise your product before the turn of the century (and television) and that was to design a beautiful and colorful label."
Steve Zeigfinger

Farther south on Route 35 in Townshend, Margie Berkowitz' **(7) ANGEL FIRE EAST ANTIQUES** offers an eclectic mix of orginal-paint furniture, decorative accessories, garden equipment, signs, and weathered architectural pieces in her two barns. She also sells some jewelry and Native American items. Weekends. 365-7276. Next door and up the drive, **(8) COLT BARN ANTIQUES** takes its name from its original location in a foaling barn on the farm where Howard Graff once escaped New York City to raise Morgans. A fulltime antiques dealer now and past VADA president, Graff enthusiastically shares his delight in high-quality American 18th- and 19th-century country pieces. He showed me some iron nutcrackers, signed and dated, that were made to fit over the knee or on the leg. Other examples of early iron included bowls, a 20-gallon pot, and a cake platter made in Philadelphia. Graff can't resist a fine piece of New England folk art, so expect an assortment of weathervanes, decoys, wood carv-

Howard Graff inspects a basket at Colt Barn Antiques

ings, and paintings in this small shop. He usually has interesting furniture, too, like carpenters' work benches. This is an outstanding collection so call ahead for your convenience. 365-7574. VADA member. www.coltbarn.com

At the Townshend village green turn right on route 30. About 1/4 mile north, Marjorie and **(9) BARRETT MENSON** own the perfect showcase for their fine collection of primitives and folk art. It's the 1790 house of Revolutionary War hero Jonas Twitchell and it boasts some unusual wall paintings. Menson, who's been dealing for 17 years is proud of his period frames and framed works, which include sandpaper drawings (that were once popular with schoolgirls), reverse glass, calligraphy, and primitive oils. He always has a good stock of hooked and

braided rugs, coun-
try furniture, and
whimsies. By chance
or appointment. 365-
7020. VADA member.

Return to the vil-
lage common and
head south on route
30. Junellen Lott
stocks country and
period furniture,
and lots of glass,
china, silver, and
quilts in a large
attractive space at
(10) HARMONY-

Barrett Menson shows off an early wall mural in his 1790 home/shop

VILLE ANTIQUES. 365-7679. Drive farther south on this ser-
pentine road and, if it's a Sunday, you'll see cars parked at the
Original Newfane Flea Market. It claims to be the oldest and
largest open-air mart in Vermont. May-Oct.

Newfane is one of New England's most photographed shires.
The entire gorgeous village is listed on the National Register of
Historic Places. So park your wheels and take a walk around the
manicured common with its fountains, the white pillared
Windham County courthouse, and the steepled Congregational
Church. On Main Street, look for the "open" flag at **(11) L.B. HALL**.
If it's flying, you've a rare treat because Richard Hall is nationally
known for his museum-quality dining furniture. As a sample, he

showed me an 1810 Regency banquet table in mahogany and a set of 8 chairs to go with it. He always has a nice selection of period multiple pedestal tables, large sets of chairs, and sideboards. Also, a good selection of 18th- and 19th-century furniture and accessories. About 60 percent of his furniture is American; the rest is English, French, and Continental. Daily 10-5 May-November; at other times by appointment. 365-4810. VADA member.

Across from Richard Hall, Shirley and William Schommer at

(12) SCHOMMER ANTIQUES have been greeting customers for 33 years. Furniture and accessories are mostly Victorian in their house and in a lovely barn with posts and beams exposed. Tables are set with fine china by Limoges, Coalport, and Royal Worchester and crystal, cranberry, and Art Deco stemware. The name cards at each place are equally impressive: Oprah Winfrey, Paul Newman, Nicole Kidman. Each of these celebrities visited the shop. One of six rooms is dedicated to William's own paint-

Shirley & William Schommer of Schommer Antiques

ings, but there are paintings throughout; the smaller ones start at $300. Daily summer and fall; by appointment winter and spring. 365-7777. VADA member.

Turn right at the Old Newfane Inn, pass the Four Columns Inn on your left, and you're on West St. Joe and Carolyn Fritzinger at **(13) FRITZINGER'S ANTIQUES** sell a small stock of early American country antiques and pre-Civil War militaria. Joe can show you several muskets and rifles made in the early 1800s. He likes to buy pieces in their original paint and had some fine examples when I last visited, such as a decorated Maine box, an 1820 tilt-top candlestand, and a green seamen's chest. You'll find choice items here—like a child's tiny desk and set of five curly maple dining room chairs—at competitive prices. 365-9312. By chance or appointment. May-Oct. At 49 West St., Ray Bates (aka **(14) THE BRITISH CLOCKMAKER**) restores and sells antique clocks, music boxes, and automata by appointment. Bates is a Master Clockmaker trained in Europe; his son Richard is his apprentice. Together they work to bring museum-quality timepieces back to life. 365-7770. www.thebritishclockmaker.com.

"My mission is to save as many of these antique clocks as I can, to bring them back to their original mechanical integrity—using all of the same techniques and materials from their period—and hope that someone will maintain that tradition long after I am gone."
Ray Bates

A half-mile south of the Newfane common on route 30, watch for **(15) JACK WINNER ANTIQUES** on the right. Jack and wife Gillian seek out period country and formal furniture in America and on the Continent. My favorite was a Swedish flame birch stepback hutch made in the 1890s. It stood next to an unusually

"During the long Vermont winters Gillian and I like to decorate sap buckets, crocks, and other Americana, which we sell in the shop." Jack Winner

pristine set of maple splat-back, cane-bottomed chairs. They also collect equestrian antiques like hunting prints, Victorian horse tack, and brass pieces called "martingales." Their inventory, nicely arranged in five barn rooms, includes brass, copper, china, toleware, quilts, hooked rugs, and fine and folk art. Thurs.-Mon. 10-5. 365-7215. www.winnerantiques.com. VADA member.

A mile and a half farther south on the right is the **(16) VILLAGE WORKSHOP**, where you'll find early tin pieces as well as classic and country antiques. Alta Sibley says "If the flag is flying we're open." Usually 10:30-4:30. 365-4653. Next door to the Sibleys, Judith Agule's shop, **(17) ANTIQUITIES**, boasts an eclectic mix of furniture and decorative pieces, such as an 1880 Canadian prayer stand in maple and white pine and a Hungarian painted shelf and trunk. A handsome Victorian pier mirror with

Judith Agule of Antiquities

handcast gesso border stands about 9 feet tall. Agule is drawn to the fancy as well as the funky, and they are all well presented in this modern gallery. Daily yearround. 365-4010.

PLACES TO STAY

CHESTER. INN VICTORIA keeps the British tradition alive by serving high tea in a drawing room filled with period antiques. Innkeepers Jack and Janet Burns offer a more modern hot-water infusion with their outdoor hot tub. Seven elegant guestrooms and suites feature queensize beds with lace-edged sheets and handcarved headboards, Victorian fainting couches, and fireplaces. They are each described on an extensive Website at www.innvictoria.com. Rates range from $110-$195. 875-4288 or 800 732-4288. 321 Main St. on the village green.

NEWFANE. THE FOUR COLUMNS INN offers 15 sunny rooms and four suites in a restored 1832 Greek Revival mansion close to the village common at 230 West Street. Gorty and Pam Baldwin traded the Big Apple for innkeeping duties and the result is pure hedonism (if such is possible). Pool swimming and hiking. $110-$240 includes breakfast. Their dining room is also a standout, where chef Greg Parks' dinner entrees cost $20-$26. 365-7713 or (800) 787-6633.

SOUTH NEWFANE. THE INN AT SOUTH NEWFANE is the creation of Dawn and Neville Cullen, a beautifully appointed 1840 Federal home on the Dover Road between Newfane and South Dover. Guests have been known to slide into rockers on the wide back porch and drift into oblivion—for days. Acres of meadow shaded by weeping willows and a swim pond ensure tranquillity. Six rooms range from $85-$130, including breakfast and lots of lawn sports. 348-7191 or (877) 548-7191. For detailed directions to the inn, check www.innatsouthnewfane.com.

PLACES TO EAT

SAXTONS RIVER. THE INN AT SAXTONS RIVER serves lunch, dinner, and Sunday brunch in a Victorian setting. Chef Tom Hickey's a la carte dinner menu always features a veggie special; most entrees cost $15.95. Many dine here as a prelude to a performance at the Saxton's River Playhouse. Popular piano bar on Fri. and Sat. 27 Main St. 869-2110.

TOWNSHEND. THE TOWNSHEND COUNTRY INN on route 30 offers great value in a cozy, family atmosphere. Dinner entrees cost from

$7.95-$12.95; Sunday brunch $9.95. This is a local favorite on Saturday nights. Daily except Wed. 365-4141.

NEWFANE. Chef Eric Weindl serves French-Swiss patés, escargots, Chateaubriand, beef Bordelaise, smoked duck breast, and other delicacies in the quaint **OLD NEWFANE INN.** Cocktails and a discriminating wine list. $18-$29. 6-9:30. Closed Mon. 365-4427 or 800 784-4427. www.oldnewfaneinn.com.

SOUTH NEWFANE. INN AT SOUTH NEWFANE. Dinner entrees prepared by Neville Cullen range from $12-$22. They might include India Green Curry, Steak au Poivre, and Saltimbocca with a slice of Double Chocolate Mousse for dessert. 5:30-9. July 4 though foliage Thurs-Tues.; off-season Thurs-Sun. (See above).

TRAVEL DIARY

TRAVEL DIARY

APPENDICES

WHAT EXACTLY IS AN ANTIQUE?
by Bob Brooke

(Brooke is a Pennsylvania-based freelance writer.)

To anyone who browses antique shops these days the question "What is an antique?" seems to have many answers. Side by side with ancient-looking furniture and old-fashioned china, browsers may find ruffled pink glass and souvenir spoons, no older than themselves. The problem bewilders dealers as well as buyers.

In 1930 the U.S. Government ruled that objects had to be at least a 100 years old to be classified as antiques, so they could be admitted duty free into the U.S. But that was a legislative tax decision. Since then antiques have often been defined as objects made before 1830.

In Europe, items as recent as that seem quite young. In contrast with a classic Roman head, an 18th-century chair is modern. Antique shops in European cities are often called "antiquities" shops. Except for Indian relics and a few Spanish buildings in the Southwest, the oldest American antiques are but 300 years old.

Yet Americans experience the same contrast in their shops. To a New Englander who knows the pine furniture of Pilgrim days, a Victorian sofa doesn't seem antique. But in Nebraska or Oregon it does, because it represents the earliest furnishings in that region. The age of antiques seems to vary relative to their environment. And so the perception of "What is antique?" changes from region to region and one part of the world to another.

Americans often count among their antiques machine-made items as well as those made by hand. Most of these were made later than 1830. That date does, however, serve as a dividing line between the age of craftsmanship and the machine age.

Legends grow on antiques the way moss grows on trees. As a family heirloom is passed from one generation to the next, its history is embellished. A spinning wheel made in 1820 becomes the spinning wheel brought over on the Mayflower. A bed crafted in 1840 becomes the bed George Washington slept in. But while the personal associations of heirlooms add to their interest, they can't be relied upon to place their date and source. Not every old piece has a pedigree or a maker's mark or label, but every one has characteristics that identify it and make it valuable to someone else. The secret of where and when and by whom it was made is in its material, its design, and its workmanship. So an antique is what the collector knows or perceives it to be. Nothing more.

SLEUTHING COUNTRY FURNITURE
by Lisa Mullenneaux

Repairs, restoration, and refinishing can all reduce the value of an old piece. Here are a few things antiques detectives look for:

•The smell of fresh paint or varnish: even a whiff should make you suspicious of new work.

•Wear: do visible surfaces feel smooth and do drawers, pulls, and latches show the effects of 150 years of opening and shutting?

•Craftsmanship: Is the wood all the same thickness? It shouldn't be. Hand-planed wood is irregular. Are the surfaces that don't show—backs, insides, and bottoms—finished? They shouldn't be if the piece is in its original condition. Early craftsmen were too frugal to waste finishes on surfaces that don't show. Are there extraneous holes? The wood was probably used for something else and has been "recycled." Do the nails or screws show age and has 100 years of oxidizing discolored the wood around them? If the nail and its hole is new, so is the furniture.

•Price: If the piece is priced far below market value, don't assume you've found a "sleeper." It's usually a sign that the piece is fake or has been heavily restored.

BEGINNING A BOOK COLLECTION
by Jane Adelson

*(Jane and Richard Adelson own Antiquarian Booksellers
in North Pomfret, 457-2608)*

Your book collection should grow out of your own personal interests. That gives you an advantage because you already have knowledge of the field. My husband, Richard, for example, has collected bird books throughout his life. He is an avid "birder." Today he is an expert on John J. Audubon books. Bookseller Justin Schiller, as a child, collected editions of *The Wizard of Oz*. Many years later when he sold his collection at Swann Galleries in New York City, the catalog of the sale became one of the best references on "Oz" material. My own interest is in children and their books. I collected children's and illustrated books before I entered the bookselling business.

Once you have identified your personal interests, you will want to narrow the scope of your collection. For example, do you want to buy all the works of Lewis Carroll, even his math books? Or do you want to specialize in all editions of *Alice in Wonderland*? Or just the first editions of all the illustrated books of *Alice in Wonderland*?

Then decide if you want to collect books to read or as an investment. This hobby can become an obsession so base your decision on what you can afford. Books just for reading can be inexpensive. In terms of resale, the best investment is to find perfect first editions with their dust wrappers, if that's how they were published.

For information about the Vermont Antiquarian Booksellers

Association, contact president Gary Austin 800-556-3727, or visit VABA's Website at www.valley.net/~vaba. VABA sponsors two book fairs in April and August. Other important resources are the Antiquarian Booksellers Association of America at www:abaa.org/; Bibliofind.com at www.bibliofind.com/; Advanced Book Exchange, which is the largest site for used and rare books, at www.abebooks.com; and Alibris at www.alibris.com, which acts as a middleman between dealers and buyers.

TALES OF ANTIQUES "PICKERS"
by René A. Vallee

(An excerpt from his forthcoming book Prof. Vallee's Den of Antiquity: Tales of a Vermont Antique Trader)

A well-stocked antiques shop is in itself a "collection." One question owners frequently are asked is "where do you get your inventory?" The sources are varied: auctions, inheritances, estate sales, yard sales, other antique shops, container imports, and, of course, the "pickers."

For those who don't know, the "pickers" are people who for some reason choose not to have a retail establishment but instead are in the antiques business "for the hunt." They provide shops with merchandise. As a group they are colorful. Some are nomadic wanderers who take weeks and even years to complete their routes.

Invariably I pay the pickers more than I would pay for identical material that I might find because picker merchandise is delivered to my door. To a shop owner, that's wonderful as inventories dwindle at mid-season.

My shop, Vallee's Den of Antiquity in Grand Isle, VT, was started in the 1940s by Lou and Velva McGarity. Several of the pickers who stop by now have been doing so since the original owners were here. Two of them arrive each spring with their old Lincoln brimming with "treasures." Abe and I chat while Zelda sets forth the merchandise. They tend to bring upscale glassware because it takes up little room in their car. "We sell about $150 worth a day," explains Abe. "It pays for our gas, our room, and our food."

These people are hard bargainers, and they "do the dance" with the zestfulness of people 50 years younger. By the way, Abe turned 90 last summer and Zelda must be close behind.

Don also dealt with the McGaritys. Now in his mid-70s, he never got a driver's license. He claims he began selling antiques from a bicycle when he was 16. He gets much of his stock by scouring obituaries and telling widows he can help with their "current dilemma."

Joe and Freida are pickers who work in a circle from Troy, NY, to Vermont. They show up four times a year, dealing in lower-end (pricewise), but interesting, merchandise. Last year they sold us a wonderful collection of *Collier's* magazine, a terrific collection of *Police Gazette*, and some FBI "wanted" photos, along with 50 circus posters in various states of decomposition. We thought we'd paid way too much until a customer paid handsomely for just one circus poster. It was Beattie Brothers "Big Otto" from 1925 or so.

A favorite picker hails from Australia by way of Montreal. He usually has his little girl, Sara, with him. Recently divorced and usually broke, he buys things from flea markets in Montreal and hawks them, spending time with his daughter in the process. I never know what he will bring.

Usually he arrives in a brief "Speedo" on the way to the beach, so my customers get a floorshow. And he's not above trying to sell things directly to my women customers, right in my shop. If it were anyone else, I would halt the practice, but he looks just like Errol Flynn and has the personality of Cary Grant, and my customers will not likely forget where this happened, soooo....

As I write this article, I glance over the wall and see a wonderful French Impressionist landscape that I got from his car trunk four years ago for $37! "Let the dance continue."

Another favorite picker is a college boy named Brad, who usually shows up with his Dad. A junior at the University of Texas, he has been picking since he was 10. His dad says he hasn't had to pay a dime for tuition. Brad sells his Vermont findings to a dozen shops in the Houston area.

A trash collector is another source. Most of his pickings are from some junk pile, but that doesn't make them any less desirable. One person's trash.... Recently this gentleman brought in a great "horned chair." It sold in two days to a very happy customer.

But not all picker stories have happy endings. Last year a seemingly sweet old lady showed up at my shop. She must have been close to 80. She had a collection of 105 little Red Rose Tea Wades and wanted $2 each. The shop was packed with customers, so I told her to set them out. She did.

After I finished with the customers, I looked at the figurines, but the light was not working where she had them set up, so I told her I would get another bulb. She replied that she didn't have time and would I just give her the money as she was running late because she had waited for my customers, etc., etc.

I gave her the money and she left...quickly. Later I inspected the figures. Each was badly chipped and had been painted with fingernail polish of the appropriate color to mask the flaws. Done in by Granny and her Winnebago! To make matters worse, there was nothing wrong with the light bulb. It had been unscrewed! (I wish I could have said the same for myself.)

ANNUAL ANTIQUES SHOWS

June: Weathersfield Center, 263-5487
             Shelburne Classic Auto Festival, 658-1827

July: Northfield Quilt Festival, 485-7092
             North Hero, 372-5357
             Craftsbury Common, 655-0006
             Manchester Village (Hildene), 362-1788),
             Stratton Classic Car Show, 1-800-STRATTON

August: Pomfret (VABA Book Auction and Fair), 457-2608
             Stowe Classic Car Show, 426-3265
             Chester, 484-5942
             Thetford, 785-4361

September: Manchester Village (Hildene), 207-767-3967
             Manchester Center (VADA), 365-7574
             Ludlow, 717-259-9480
             Rutland, 603-569-0000
             Bromley, 457-3437

October: Weston, 824-4100
             Manchester Village (Hildene), 362-1788)

TRAVEL RESOURCES

GENERAL INFORMATION: Call the Vermont Dept. of Tourism and Marketing at 828-3237 or (800) VERMONT or visit its Website at www.1-800-vermont.com. You can request a travel kit, check special events, book a room, or get a weather report.

REGIONAL INFORMATION: Call these toll-free numbers:
Lake Champlain islands and northwestern VT (800) 262-5226
Stowe/Smuggler's Notch (877) 247-8693
Burlington and vicinity (877) 686-5253
Central VT, including Barre, Montpelier, and
 Waterbury (877) 887-4968
Middlebury and Vergennes (800) 733-8376
Rutland and the Killington area (800) 756-8880
Woodstock (888) 848-4199
Quechee (888) 663-6656
Bennington, Manchester, Dorset (877) 768-3766
Chester, Grafton, Townshend, Newfane (877) 887-2378

WELCOME CENTERS: Look for Vermont state welcome centers along Route 4A, I-91, I-93, and I-89. Chambers of commerce in towns throughout the state also run information centers.

LODGING AND RESTAURANTS: The Vermont Lodging and Restaurant Association runs www.visitvt.com, which allows you to search by map, name, or city and then make a reservation. The Chamber's Vermont Traveler's Guidebook and Winter Guide lists inns, restaurants, and local attractions by town. To order, call (802) 223-3443 or find them online at www.vtchamber.com.

MAPS: www.travel-vermont.com. Vermont's official state map has a wealth of travel tips, from museums to covered bridges.

BROCHURES: VADA's directory of members is called *Antiquing in Vermont*. To order a copy, send a double-stamped, self-addressed business-size envelope to: James Harley, 88 Reading Farms Rd., Reading, VT 05062. The brochure is also available in many shops. VADA's Website is www.antweb.com/vada.

VABA's directory of members is called *Old Books*. To order, write: Tom Twetten, Craftsbury Antiquarian Books, PO Box 111, Craftsbury Common, VT 05827 or call 802 586-2495. Their Website is www.valley.net/~vaba

The Antique Hunters Guide to Route 7 brochure is available by calling (802) 496-3062.

NEWSPAPERS: *Vermont Antique Times* is available in many shops and by calling 362-3149 or (800) 542-4224. Also, check out the *Maine Antique Digest* (207) 832-4888, *New Hampshire Antique Monthly* (603) 755-4568, *New England Antiques Journal* (800) 432-3505, and *Northeast* (518) 828-1616.

MAGAZINES: *Vermont Life* and *Vermont* feature the state's major attractions. *Antiques* magazine has many articles on the history of Vermont antiques.

TRAVEL BOOKS: Aiken, Kenneth. *Touring Vermont's Scenic Roads*. Down East Books, 1999.

Barna, Ed. *Covered Bridges of Vermont*. The Countryman Press, 2000.

Freidin, John. *25 Bicycle Tours in Vermont*. The Countryman Press, 1996.

Jennison, Peter. *The Roadside History of Vermont*. Mountain Press Publishing, 1989.

Rogers, Barbara R. and Stillman D. *Country Towns of Vermont*. Country Roads Press, 1998.

Scheeler, Kay and Bill. *The Best Vermont Drives*. Jasper Heights Press, 1999.

Tree, Christina and Jennison, Peter. *Vermont: An Explorer's Guide*, The Countryman Press, 1999.

ANTIQUES BOOKS: Barret, Richard C. *How to Identify Bennington Pottery*, Stephen Greene Press, 1964.

Bennington Museum, *The Best the Country Affords: Vermont Furniture 1765-1850*, 1995.

Freeman, Lisa and Fiske, John eds. *The Green Guide to Antiquing in New England*. 7th edition. Globe Pequot Press, 1999.

Osgood, Cornelius. *The Jug and Related Stoneware of Bennington*. Charles E. Tuttle, 1971.

Robinson, Charles A. *Vermont Cabinetmakers and Chairmakers Working Before 1855: A Checklist*. The Shelburne Museum, 1994.

DEALER QUICK REFERENCE GUIDE

(Y) INDICATES OPEN YEARROUND

(S) INDICATES OPEN SEASONALLY

(A) INDICATES OPEN BY APPOINTMENT ONLY.

1829 House Antiques, 644-2912, Y

American Classics, 457-4337, Y

Andrews Antiques, 352-6016, Y

Angel Fire East Antiques, 365-7276, Y

Antiques Collaborative, 296-5858, Y

Antiquities, 365-4010, Y

Architectural Salvage Warehouse, 658-5011, Y

Athens Antique Prints and the Richter Gallery, 869-2722, Y

The Barn, 388-7584, A

The Barn Antiques, 293-5512, Y

Barrett Menson Antiques, 365-7020, A

Bix Antiques, 388-2277 or 800 486-4355, S

Black Horse Farm, 484-3539, Y

The British Clockmaker, 365-7770, A

The Buggy Man Antiques Center, 635-2110, Y

The Buggy Man II, 635-7664, Y

Burlington Centre for Antiques, 985-4911, Y

Bygone Books, 862-4397, Y

Center Hill Past and Present, 362-3211, Y

The Chocolate Barn, 375-6928, Y

Clarendon House, Inc., 438-2449, A

The Clock Doctor, 235-2440, A

Colt Barn Antiques: 365-7574, Y

Comollo Antiques, 362-7188, Y

Conant Custom Brass, 658-4482 or 800 832-4482, Y

Conway's Antiques, 775-5153, Y

Country Gallery Antiques, 394-7753, Y

Country House Antiques, 446-2344, Y

The Crimson Buggy, 483-2804, Y

Danby Antiques Center, 293-9984, Y

Dr. Tom's Antiques, 388-0153, Y

Early Vermont Antiques, 244-5373, Y

East Arlington Antiques Center, 375-9607, Y

Eighth Elm Farm Antiques, 877-3218, Y

The Farm Antiques, 375-6302, A

Fitz-Gerald's, 877-2539, Y

Fonda's Antiques, 442-5985, Y

Four Corners East, 442-2612, Y

Fraser's Antiques: 457-3437, Y

Fritzinger's Antiques, 365-9312, S

Grafton Gathering Place: 875-2309, Y

Harmonyville Antiques, 365-7679, Y

It's About Time, Ltd., 985-5772, Y

Jack Winner Antiques, 365-7215, Y

Judy Pascal Antiques, 362-2004, Y

Kittell's, 635-7119, Y

L. B. Hall, 365-4810, A

The Lamp Shop, 864-6782, Y

The Lamplighter, Y

Lee B. Pirkey, 247-3277, Y

Liberty Hill Antiques: 484-7710, S

Maiden Lane, 362-2004, Y

Marie Miller American Quilts, 867-5969, Y

Martha Lewis Antiques, 244-8919, Y

Meander Bookshop, 362-0700, S

Mel Siegel Antiques, 635-2000, S

Michael and Lucinda Seward Antiques, 483-6434, A

Middlebury Antique Center, Inc., 388-6229 or 800-339-6229, Y

Middlestone Antiques, 867-4448, Y

Mill Brook Antiques: 484-5942, Y

Norman Gronning Antiques, 375-6376, A

North Country Books, 862-6413, Y

Nutting House Antiques, 247-3302 or 800 870-9866, S

The Old Cow's Tail Antiques, 362-3363, Y

Old Dog Antiques, 457-9800, Y

Old Spa Shop Antiques, 235-2366, A

Old Tyme Shop Antiques, 446-2828, A

Paraphernalia, 362-2421, S

Peg and Judd Gregory, 867-4407, Y

Phyllis Carlson, 867-4510, S

Pleasant Street Books, 457-4050, Y

Polo Antiques, 457-5837, Y

Praxis, 457-2396, Y

Rosebud Antiques at Houston Farm, 253-2333, Y

Schommer Antiques, 365-7777, Y

Schoolhouse Antiques, 869-2332, Y

Shelburne Village Antiques: 985-1447, Y

Sign of the Raven, 869-2500, S

Sir Richard's Antique Center, 244-8879, Y

Smuggler's Notch Antique Center, 644-8321, Y

Somerville House Antiques, 985-3431, Y

Stone Block Antiques, 877-3359, Y

Stonewalls Antiques, 447-1628, S

Stowe Antiques Center, 253-9875 or 888 802-5441, Y

Sylvan Hill Antiques: 875-3954, A

Upstairs Antiques, 859-8966, Y

Vallees Den of Antiquity, 372-8324, S

Victorian House Antiques, 635-9549, Y

The Village Barn Antiques, 644-2030, Y

Village Workshop, 365-4653, Y

Vincent J. Fernandez, 985-2275, Y

Washburn Antiques, 877-1558, Y

Whistle Stop Antiques, 951-9189, Y

Wigren-Barlow, 457-2453, Y

William Austin's Antiques, 875-3032 or 877 447-5268, Y

Yellow House Antiques: 484-7799, A

INDEX OF TOWNS BY ITINERARY

Arlington	Itinerary 1
Athens	Itinerary 6
Bennington	Itinerary 1
Brandon	Itinerary 2
Burlington	Itinerary 3
Chester	Itinerary 6
Clarendon Springs	Itinerary 2
Danby	Itinerary 2
Dorset	Itinerary 1
East Arlington	Itinerary 1
East Middlebury	Itinerary 2
Ferrisburgh	Itinerary 3
Grafton	Itinerary 6
Grand Isle	Itinerary 3
Harmonyville	Itinerary 6
Hyde Park	Itinerary 4
Jeffersonville	Itinerary 4
Johnson	Itinerary 4
Manchester	Itinerary 1
Middlebury	Itinerary 2
Middletown Springs	Itinerary 2
Morrisville	Itinerary 4
Newfane	Itinerary 6
Pittsford	Itinerary 2
Quechee	Itinerary 5
Reading	Itinerary 5

INDEX OF TOWNS BY ITINERARY

Rupert	Itinerary 1
Rutland	Itinerary 2
Salisbury	Itinerary 2
Saxtons River	Itinerary 6
Shaftsbury	Itinerary 1
Shelburne	Itinerary 3
Smugglers' Notch	Itinerary 4
South Newfane	Itinerary 6
Stowe	Itinerary 4
Taftsville	Itinerary 5
Tinmouth	Itinerary 2
Townshend	Itinerary 6
Vergennes	Itinerary 3
Wallingford	Itinerary 2
Waterbury	Itinerary 4
Woodstock	Itinerary 5

ORDER FORM

Please send me _____copies of **Vermont Antiquing: Six Day Trips** at $9.95 a copy

New York Address? Add 8 % sales tax

Shipping: Add $2.00 for the first book and $1.00 for each additional book

I enclose a check for $_____

Send to: **The Penington Press, P.O. Box 829, New York, NY 10009-9998**

QUESTIONS? Call (212) 777-3295 and check out our Website at www.peningtonpress.com